Identity-Conscious Teaching, Learning, and Curriculum

Strategies and Activities for Inclusive Classrooms

Liza Talusan

Routledge
Taylor & Francis Group
NEW YORK AND LONDON

Designed cover image: Getty Images

First published 2027
by Routledge
605 Third Avenue, New York, NY 10158

and by Routledge
4 Park Square, Milton Park, Abingdon, Oxon, OX14 4RN

Routledge is an imprint of the Taylor & Francis Group, an informa business

ISBN: 978-1-041-32829-2 (pbk)
ISBN: 978-1-003-78473-9 (ebk)

DOI: 10.4324/9781003784739

Typeset in Palatino
by Apex CoVantage, LLC

Disclaimer:
Names in stories have been changed.

Access the Support Material: www.routledge.com/9781041328292

"*Identity-Conscious Teaching, Learning, and Curriculum* is a brilliant, practical roadmap for educators committed to joyful, identity-affirming classrooms. This book shows us how to honor and center students' identities and move from reflection to sustained action for equity."

– **Dr. Dena Simmons**, *author, scholar, and founder of LiberatED*

"Liza Talusan's work is soul work. It does not simply ask educators to think – it asks us to feel, to reckon, to remember who we are and who we have been taught to be. To become identity-conscious is not a strategy; it is an act of self-love, and like all real love, it demands truth. Her latest book, *Identity-Conscious Teaching, Learning, and Curriculum,* is a guide to joy and love, offering beautiful prompts and activities that call us to show up whole and committed to transformation. Let Liza's storytelling, coaching, and teaching guide you home. She is one of our greatest teachers."

– **Dr. Bettina Love**, *Abolitionist + Freedom Dreamer*

"Too often, we want to believe that what we teach and how we teach it are neutral processes, existing outside ourselves. Dr. Liza Talusan reminds us that we each bring a lens to them based on our identity, cultural reference points, and social privilege based on race, gender, and economics that influences our practice. In *Identity-Conscious Teaching, Learning, and Curriculum,* she offers a powerful process for leveraging identity consciousness as an engine for liberatory education that disrupts deep-rooted biases gripping our school systems."

– **Zaretta Hammond**, *teacher educator and author of* Culturally Responsive Teaching and the Brain *and* Rebuilding Students' Learning Power: Teaching for Instructional Equity and Cognitive Justice

"In her latest book, *Identity-Conscious Teaching, Learning, and Curriculum,* Dr. Liza Talusan expertly holds the flashlight for us to keep doing the good work of building knowledge, establishing a reflective practice, and most of all – taking action to build the schools our students deserve. Every bookshelf should hold space for this gem."

– **Jennifer De Leon**, *tenured professor, author of* Don't Ask Me Where I'm From, *and co-founder of Story Bridge*

Identity-Conscious Teaching, Learning, and Curriculum

When teachers and leaders implement an identity-conscious practice, they can provide a more responsive and responsible learning environment. But how do we engage in teaching, learning, and curriculum building through an identity-conscious lens?

Award-winning author Liza Talusan helps educators grapple with four key questions:

1. How does identity inform and impact my approach to teaching, learning, and curriculum?
2. How can I build a more identity-conscious teaching practice related to instruction, delivery, sequence, and engagement?
3. How can I implement a more identity-conscious classroom community focused on culturally sustaining learning, cultural practices, and asset-based learning models?
4. How can I build a more identity-conscious curriculum, scope, sequence, and source material to reflect my students' experiences?

Readers explore these questions by building knowledge on these topics, engaging in reflection about their practices, and establishing their own action plans for shaping a more inclusive and equitable environment.

Liza Talusan, PhD, is an educator, speaker, leader, writer, coach, and parent. She has over 27 years of experience in PreK-20 education and is currently a faculty member in the College of Education and Human Development at the University of Massachusetts Boston. Her book *The Identity Conscious Educator: Building Habits and Skills for a More Inclusive School*, published by Solution Tree Press, is the 2023 Gold Medal Recipient of IPPY Awards. She is also the author of *Identity-Conscious Practice in Action: Shaping Equitable Schools and Classrooms* (Routledge, 2025).

Equity and Social Justice in Education Series

Paul C. Gorski, Series Editor

Routledge's Equity and Social Justice in Education series is a publishing home for books that apply critical and transformative equity and social justice theories to the work of on-the-ground educators. Books in the series describe meaningful solutions to the racism, white supremacy, economic injustice, sexism, heterosexism, transphobia, ableism, neoliberalism, and other oppressive conditions that pervade schools and school districts.

Teaching Indigenous Studies: An Introduction for K-12 Educators
Leilani Sabzalian, Meredith McCoy, and Helen Thomas

Peacebuilding Pedagogies: Racial Justice, Dialogue, and Belonging in the Classroom
Crystena Parker-Shandal

Cultivating Critical Advocacy: A Framework for Educators of Multilingual Learners
Rebecca E. Linares and Kate Seltzer

The DEI Practitioner's Handbook: A Guide for School and District Leaders in Pursuit of Educational Justice
Erica Buchanan-Rivera

Teaching Multilingual Learners in Rural Schools: Four Movements for Educators
Maria Coady

Healing-Centered Writing in the Secondary Classroom: An Identity-Affirming and Restorative Approach
Ioanna Pettas Opidee

Multilingual Justice in Schools: Centering Multilingual Learners' Academic, Linguistic, and Socio-Cultural Experiences
Andrea Honigsfeld

Identity-Conscious Teaching, Learning, and Curriculum: Strategies and Activities for Inclusive Classrooms
Liza Talusan

Identity-Conscious Teaching, Learning, and Curriculum

When teachers and leaders implement an identity-conscious practice, they can provide a more responsive and responsible learning environment. But how do we engage in teaching, learning, and curriculum building through an identity-conscious lens?

Award-winning author Liza Talusan helps educators grapple with four key questions:

1. How does identity inform and impact my approach to teaching, learning, and curriculum?
2. How can I build a more identity-conscious teaching practice related to instruction, delivery, sequence, and engagement?
3. How can I implement a more identity-conscious classroom community focused on culturally sustaining learning, cultural practices, and asset-based learning models?
4. How can I build a more identity-conscious curriculum, scope, sequence, and source material to reflect my students' experiences?

Readers explore these questions by building knowledge on these topics, engaging in reflection about their practices, and establishing their own action plans for shaping a more inclusive and equitable environment.

Liza Talusan, PhD, is an educator, speaker, leader, writer, coach, and parent. She has over 27 years of experience in PreK-20 education and is currently a faculty member in the College of Education and Human Development at the University of Massachusetts Boston. Her book *The Identity Conscious Educator: Building Habits and Skills for a More Inclusive School*, published by Solution Tree Press, is the 2023 Gold Medal Recipient of IPPY Awards. She is also the author of *Identity-Conscious Practice in Action: Shaping Equitable Schools and Classrooms* (Routledge, 2025).

Equity and Social Justice in Education Series

Paul C. Gorski, Series Editor

Routledge's Equity and Social Justice in Education series is a publishing home for books that apply critical and transformative equity and social justice theories to the work of on-the-ground educators. Books in the series describe meaningful solutions to the racism, white supremacy, economic injustice, sexism, heterosexism, transphobia, ableism, neoliberalism, and other oppressive conditions that pervade schools and school districts.

Teaching Indigenous Studies: An Introduction for K-12 Educators
Leilani Sabzalian, Meredith McCoy, and Helen Thomas

Peacebuilding Pedagogies: Racial Justice, Dialogue, and Belonging in the Classroom
Crystena Parker-Shandal

Cultivating Critical Advocacy: A Framework for Educators of Multilingual Learners
Rebecca E. Linares and Kate Seltzer

The DEI Practitioner's Handbook: A Guide for School and District Leaders in Pursuit of Educational Justice
Erica Buchanan-Rivera

Teaching Multilingual Learners in Rural Schools: Four Movements for Educators
Maria Coady

Healing-Centered Writing in the Secondary Classroom: An Identity-Affirming and Restorative Approach
Ioanna Pettas Opidee

Multilingual Justice in Schools: Centering Multilingual Learners' Academic, Linguistic, and Socio-Cultural Experiences
Andrea Honigsfeld

Identity-Conscious Teaching, Learning, and Curriculum: Strategies and Activities for Inclusive Classrooms
Liza Talusan

This book is dedicated to those who teach with courage.

Contents

Support Material

The discussion questions at the end of each section are also compiled into a study guide that you can download and print to make it easier to discuss the book with colleagues and teams. To access the guide, go to the book product page at Routledge.com/9781041328292 and click on the link that says Support Material.

Meet the Author

Dr. Liza (LIE-zuh) Talusan (taLOOS-ahn) is an educator, speaker, leader, writer, coach, and parent. With over 30 years of experience in PreK-20 education, Liza is an engaging facilitator in conversations about diversity, anti-racism, bias, privilege, and power and creates environments that allow for people to discuss these difficult topics openly. Currently, Liza serves as Graduate Program Director of the Higher Education Doctoral Program at the University of Massachusetts Boston.

Dr. Talusan has been invited to more than 400 organizations across the country and internationally to facilitate dialogue groups, workshops, strategic planning, change management, and community-focused sessions.

Liza is the recipient of numerous awards, including "Best 40 Under 40"; NASPA Region I Mid-Level Professional Award; NASPA APIKC VIP Award; Asian Women for Health's Peer Leader Award; Promise in Action Mentoring Nominee; Network for Equity, Excellence in Education Award; the REAPA (AERA) Dissertation of the Year Award; the Harriet Buescher Lawrence Prize from Connecticut College; the Early Career Award (REAPA); the YMCA Leadership Award; and a number of institutional grants.

She earned her bachelor's degree from Connecticut College; Masters of Arts from New York University; PhD from University of Massachusetts Boston; Certificate in Human Resources; and her PCC Coaching Credentials from the Institute for Professional Excellence in Coaching.

Liza has been a guest on a number of podcasts focused on educational equity and is the new co-host for the podcast *Teaching While White*. Liza's book *The Identity Conscious Educator: Building Habits and Skills for More Inclusive Schools*, published by Solution Tree Press, is the 2023 Gold Medal Recipient of IPPY Awards.

Liza's top five StrengthsQuest themes are *Achiever, Maximizer, Discipline, Activator, and Connectedness.* She is someone who is driven, results-oriented, effective and organized, engages others to reach their potential, and practices the principles of community and human connection.

- Instagram and Threads: @ltalusan
- Facebook: @LTCAC

Acknowledgements

I am very privileged to teach at a university, in a department, and with a program that not only thinks about but also actively works towards educational justice. I realize this is not the case at every school, particularly during this current social and political climate. Therefore, thank you to the students and colleagues at the University of Massachusetts Boston, College of Education and Human Development, Higher Education Program, for continuing to fight for equitable and joyous educational communities.

Thank you to Paul Gorksi, Lauren Davis, and all at Routledge's Equity in Education series for your advocacy and careful guidance of this book. I am grateful for the opportunities you have provided me over the years to contribute in meaningful ways to our field.

Thank you to my parents, Eduardo and Araceli, along with the best siblings (Mary, Grace, Paul, and Jonathan), their partners, and my niblings. People often ask me what it is like to have a family of such brilliance. Easy – it's dope.

For years, I was a part of a community called Saturday Writing Team. Though it was a tough lesson in trust, integrity, and collaboration, I am grateful for the friendships and family I have made on that journey and the affirmation that there are people who I can trust as a writer and scholar. Thank you for years of encouragement and support. Thank you to all the people I should never sit next to in meetings. Thank you to courageous practitioners and scholars whom I have the privilege of calling family. I do this work in community with you. A special shout out to Dr. Kipp Trieu who helped me to think thorugh the rubrics found in this book.

My Pilipino *kapwa* always keeps it real. Thanks to all those who are in the movement of *isang bagsak* and the allies who show up alongside us. "When one rises, we all rise." Thank you to so many Asian American and Pacific Islander scholars who shaped how I think and move thorugh this world. And thank you to all of those who work in solidarity to dismantle oppression in our classrooms, schools, and communities.

Thank you to Jorge, who models each day what good teaching can do. Thank you to Joli, Jay, and Evan – I am proud of you beyond measure. You continue to push me to be better, to think more critically, and to live a life of integrity. I write these books to work towards a better educational system that is inspired by you. Thank you for sharing your educational stories with me and ways we can make things better. Thank you to Milo, Oreo, and KoD for our long walks, reconnecting with nature, and keeping me humble.

Finally, thank you to all the teachers, leaders, and advocates who do this work every single day. We have faced so many challenges in our field, and your dedication in the face of obstacles – political, social, and institutional – continues to give me faith that we will be all right.

Introduction

Hit, hit, clap. Hit, hit, clap. Hit, hit, clap. The sound of the large bamboo poles against the gymnasium floor echoed throughout the room during a performance of the *tinikling* – the traditional Filipino dance inspired by the movement of the small *tikling* bird jumping in and out of tree branches and avoiding traps set by farmers. In the *tinikling,* skilled dancers move in between these rhythmic claps of the poles, avoiding getting their ankles caught and demonstrating quick jumping and hopping movements. During my childhood, from the audience, I watched my peers who attended Filipino cultural schools perform this dance at festivals. As I grew older, I watched college cultural clubs and organizations perform updated hip-hop versions of the *tinikling* dance and included acrobatics, such as cartwheels and aerial moves, in between the rhythmic claps.

For a few reasons, my parents never sent my siblings and me to Filipino cultural school – mostly because it was too far from our home in the suburbs, and they were already shuttling five children around to other weekend activities, such as music lessons, soccer, basketball, and hockey. But there was always a part of me that regretted not going to cultural school – not knowing my home language, dances, or customs of my people and only being on the sidelines of these events.

Of all the cultural dances that are performed at these shows, the *tinikling* is the only dance that I know how to do. But I did not learn the *tinikling* from Filipino cultural school experience or other cultural organizations. I learned how to dance the *tinikling* from my 5th-grade physical education teacher, Mr. Trombley, in my small town outside of Boston. Mr. Trombley was a tall,

DOI: 10.4324/9781003784739-1

middle-aged, blond-haired, blue-eyed teacher who taught 5th- and 6th-grade physical education. From what I remember, Mr. Trombley lost the toes on one of his feet and showed us how the top of his sneaker folded where his toes should have been. This fact became a core memory of my middle school years.

One day, Mr. Trombley walked into the gymnasium with a set of bamboo poles that were ten feet tall. "Wait, I know those sticks," I thought. "It can't be. Those can't be *tinikling* poles. Maybe he is using them to make an obstacle course. Maybe those are just props for an activity. Maybe these are weird pole-vaulting sticks or something. Maybe . . . maybe." Mr. Trombley laid the set of bamboo poles on the gymnasium floor and announced, "Class, we are going to learn a dance from the Philippines called the *tinikling*." Every 5th grader groaned when he said the word "dance," and I immediately wanted to run and hide.

But because middle schoolers thought Mr. Trombley was cool (remember, the sneaker story), he stood at the front of the room, told us to line up into rows, and began teaching us moves of the *tinikling*. He showed us how to tap our right foot twice to the side, lift our foot, and then set it back down and tap twice again. *Hit, hit, clap. Hit, hit, clap.* Once we could do that move without falling, Mr. Trombley taught us how to hop across the bamboo sticks in rhythm to avoid getting our ankles caught. *Hit, hit, clap. Hit, hit, clap.* Before long, the all-White (except for me) 5th-grade class of Easton Middle School was performing the national dance of the Philippines. And we were having fun!

In my K-12 schooling, I would never again experience this kind of joy related to my ethnic and racial identity. I would never encounter information about the Philippines in any culturally reflective way. I would never see my classmates participate – and enjoy – part of my cultural heritage that I loved so much. I know it is not possible to teach about every country, every ethnic group, or every identity, but I do know what I felt like when my identity was included at school. The feeling I experienced during that unit in middle school physical education class stayed with me forever. The way that Mr. Trombley so intentionally and enthusiastically taught an entire group of White 5th-grade students a cultural dance brought me such joy. And the absence I felt the rest of my educational experience is what shaped my own teaching, learning, and curricular practice. As a teacher, I was committed to creating that same joy, enthusiasm, and care for my students. I was going to be the Mr. Trombley for all the other students who felt left out of teaching, learning, and curriculum. I was going to be the teacher that my younger self needed.

I have heard the phrase "People don't always remember what you teach, but they remember how you made them feel." I am not sure if Mr. Trombley already had the *tinikling* as part of his physical education curriculum, which included dodgeball, military marching formations, and calisthenics, but I want to believe he had a moment and thought, "You know what, I can do something here." I will never know. But I do remember how he made me feel. As an Asian American 5th grader at a nearly all-White, Irish, and Italian school in the mid-1980s, Mr. Trombley made me feel like I was a part of something special. He made learning personal. And, over 40 years later, my body and heart remember every dance step of the *tinikling*. Thank you, Mr. Trombley. How you made me feel in middle school is one of the reasons why I care so deeply about teaching, learning, and curriculum from an identity-conscious lens and why I am motivated to work with other teachers to do the same.

All in One Place

As educators, we can be overwhelmed with the vast number of resources available related to teaching, learning, and curriculum. While there were many independent resources that discussed teaching *or* learning *or* curriculum, there were few resources that addressed the impact and intersections of all three. Further, there were few resources that considered how identity informed and impacted the processes of teaching, learning, and curriculum taken together. There are many incredible authors, scholars, and practitioners who helped shape my own understanding of teaching, learning, and curriculum and allowed me the opportunity to build upon their work through the lens of an identity-conscious practice. In particular, the work of Zaretta Hammond, Bettina Love, Dena Simmons, and Gholdy Muhammad allowed me to do a deep dive into my own teaching, learning, and curriculum work. I highly recommend using their texts in each of the areas of teaching, learning, and curriculum. They, too, integrate an identity-conscious lens into their work, and I wrote this text to be a place that brings all four of these ideas (identity-conscious teaching, learning, and curriculum) into one place.

I am sensitive to the current climate of K-12 teaching, where educators are being asked to do more with less – less time, less resources, and less support. The current K-12 faculty I connected with wanted opportunities to deepen their learning, to examine the intersections of identity, teaching, learning, and curriculum, and to continue to build the habits and skills of more inclusive and equitable engagement; but they needed to do it in a way that would fit into their faculty meetings, department meetings, or the brief professional development session. They wanted a resource they could read, discuss, reflect upon, and identify productive and positive action in their work that did not take away from their current prep time. They wanted to be able to integrate the work immediately after a discussion. Current educators pushed for a book where they could build knowledge and learn more about the contexts of teaching, learning, and curriculum; engage with structured prompts to reflect upon their practices; and have room to develop strategies and actions for sustaining a teaching, learning, and curriculum through an identity-conscious lens.

Therefore, while it is impossible to be "everything to everyone," this book is an attempt to bring together so many needs in one place. This text is helpful to those who may just be starting on their teaching and learning journey while also a critical resource for existing teachers and school leaders who are looking to define, assess, and reshape their current practices. This resource is also helpful to instructional coaches, teaching and learning offices, and those who are accountable for curriculum development by providing rubrics and assessments they can use to give concrete feedback about implementing an identity-conscious practice. As learning communities, schools will find this book helpful to their faculty, staff, and students as they build knowledge, engage in reflection, and create actionable changes to teaching, learning, and curriculum to action in ways that can be done steadily throughout the academic year.

Readers of this book will find a familiar rhythm and flow that I used in my previous book: build knowledge, engage in reflection, and move to action.

- Build knowledge: What do we need to know?
- Engage in reflection: What does this have to do with me?
- Move to action: What am I supposed to do now?

In Part I, we explore the foundations of an identity-conscious practice. We engage in exercises to help us raise our level of understanding of how identity might inform and impact how we act, interact, and see the world around us. Readers will learn how an identity-conscious practice serves as a foundation for efforts related to diversity, equity, and inclusion and shape community initiatives rooted in this awareness.

In Part II, we begin to look at the theories that inform ethical and equitable teaching practices. We dive into the act of decolonizing teaching practices, explore the ways in which deficit lens teaching impacts students, and consider how we can shift to asset-based models. We are introduced to a reflective practice for faculty to engage with meaningful relationships and teaching.

In Part III, we explore the theories related to learning, such as culturally responsive pedagogy and culturally sustaining practices, and how they contribute to positive learning experiences. In this section, readers will engage with different practices related to learning, particularly through a trauma-informed lens.

In Part IV, we examine how curricular efforts can shape greater belonging in the classroom. From an identity-conscious lens, we will explore how existing curricular efforts can be edited, changed, or adjusted to better reflect the research related to culturally responsive curriculum.

In Part V, we bring it all together. This chapter provides the reader opportunities to reflect on the previous work and demonstrate how to move identity-conscious teaching, learning, and curriculum forward in their practice.

I am grateful that you chose this book to use on your own journey. I hope this book serves as a helpful way for you to build knowledge and learn more about the different theories and approaches to identity-conscious teaching, learning, and curriculum (ICTLC); to engage in reflection and deeply connect your own experiences to this work; and to move to action and create meaningful steps towards greater inclusion and equity.

Part I

An Introduction to an Identity-Conscious Practice

Key elements

- Why does identity matter in schools?
- How does a deficit lens impact our approaches to identity and education?
- What are the foundations of an identity-conscious practice?

Throughout my school experiences, I was an average student. I was not at the top of my class nor at the bottom, but I hovered somewhere in the middle. Despite my mediocre performance, I was placed into honors level courses in high school. My classmates seemed to grasp the knowledge and skills easily, earning As on their assignments, while I was struggling to keep up with my generous C+s.

I always wondered why I was placed in these honors-level classes. On one hand, I had an older sister who was in all honors classes and who did incredibly well in our small-town public school. Maybe teachers saw the similar last name and assumed that I was also smart and talented in the classroom, just like her. Maybe they saw that I was Asian American, and leaning into stereotypes such as the model minority myth, they assumed I should be in honors classes. Maybe it was that I was personable, friendly, outgoing, and in general, teachers liked me. I can confidently say that my grades – yes, one measure of achievement – were not the reason I was in honors courses.

DOI: 10.4324/9781003784739-2

I quickly learned that being in honors classes referred to the pace at which the class moved. Honors students were expected to complete more assignments during the week, read more, and write in a more sophisticated and critical manner than other levels. We were supposed to be able to comprehend complicated material and read proficiently. I, however, always seemed to lack the intellectual maturity of my classmates. I always felt two steps behind them. My essays lacked analysis and synthesis. My answers were always basic-level responses. And my short-answer responses barely made it past the concrete phase.

Though I was not as critical a thinker as the rest of my class, I did love to read. In 10th-grade English class, I remember coming to school so excited after an assigned reading of Edgar Allen Poe's *The Murders in the Rue Morgue*. I loved mysteries and suspense, and this book had captured my attention. I came to school excited to talk about the story and participate in class. As we waited for the teacher to begin, I turned to some of my classmates and said, "I loved last night's reading! The *orangu-rangu* was so wild!" My classmates started to laugh, "The story about *what?*" my classmate Jeremy asked. "You know, the *orangu-rangu*," I replied. They were laughing so hard at me, it took a minute for them to catch their collective breaths. "What is wrong with you? It's not *orangu-rangu*, Liza. It's *orangutan* – you know, like the monkey?" As an insecure and embarrassed 15-year-old, I quickly replied, "Of course, I know it's an orangutan. I was just being funny!" I sat in my seat and did not say a word the entire class.

It was clear to my classmates, and to me, that I was the weakest one in the class. Over the years, I lost confidence in myself and stopped raising my hand. I never volunteered to solve an answer on the board or read aloud a passage from a text. On the rare occasion when I did ask for more clarification or help from the teacher, my classmates would roll their eyes and whisper, "She just doesn't get it. What is she even doing here?"

What I lacked in academic prowess, I tried to make up for in personality. While I was friendly and outgoing, no one wanted to be my partner for labs or group projects because they knew they would have to carry me intellectually. I was always willing to outwork anyone, but I always failed to understand what we were doing. While everyone was applying to Ivy League colleges and Tier 1 schools, I was rejected by every school but one – the local college where I had spent six summers at music camp. My guidance counselors simply approved my inappropriate list of colleges – ones that I never should have applied to given my grades – and yet no one seemed surprised when my mailbox was filled with rejection letters.

As an Asian American growing up in a predominantly White town, I was always aware of identity. I was especially aware of my racial identity in my classes – as only one of three Asian Americans in my entire grade and usually the only one in any given class. I always believed I was not smart, not good enough at school, and honestly just too dumb to understand what was happening in class. Yet everyone told me that "Asians were smart" and "Asians were good at math and science" and "Asians get As." It never occurred to me, until I entered into my own teaching career, that maybe my experiences of feeling less than were a combination of things: 1) I was not at the right placement level in my classes; 2) I was likely placed in advanced classes due to stereotypes about Asian Americans as high-achieving students; 3) I often felt ashamed in class because I did not understand concepts as quickly as my classmates, which led me to shut down, feel discouraged, and unmotivated to learn; and 4) my teachers, if they recognized my struggle, did nothing to intervene or talk with me about my experiences.

In my adulthood and teaching career, I was reminded that "An anxious brain will have difficulty learning." I realized this, 40 years later, that my anxiety about learning, about being smart, and trying to keep up with my classmates got in the way of my learning experience. Coupled with a curriculum that was always centered on European histories, contributions, and successes, I never saw myself, my culture, and my people in the curriculum and spent years learning about others. Through selected texts and the teachers who influenced my growth and development, I grew up being told that Europeans were better and smarter than other people in history and that inferiority carried through to how I thought of myself in class. A combination of lack of representation in the curriculum coupled with feeling like an outsider, I always felt less than.

It took years for me to unravel how my schooling and educational experiences shaped some of these deficit lenses. Writing about effective teaching, learning, curriculum, and identity strategies is, in some way, my apology to the younger version of me who did not experience an educational environment in which teaching, learning, and curriculum were rooted in identity-conscious practices. I often ask myself, "What would have been different if my teachers were more conscious of how identity showed up in the classroom? What would have been different if the teachers knew how much their own identities shaped what they taught and how they taught?"

Here is where our identity-conscious journey begins. This section serves as a primer for how to build an identity-conscious practice. If you have not already read *The Identity-Conscious Educator: Building Habits and Skills for More Inclusive Schools* (Solution Tree Press, 2022), I do recommend reading it to begin this journey. In this book, we will build on some of the scaffolding that is provided in that book. We will be exploring the impact of identity-consciousness on teaching, learning, and curriculum (TLC) and how we can build better habits and skills that result in greater support for our students.

What Is an Identity-Conscious Practice?

Identity informs and impacts how we act, interact, and see the world around us (Talusan, 2022). Building an identity-conscious practice provides us the opportunity to be curious – to ask *why and how* identity shapes our behaviors, our relationships, and our thoughts about the world. An identity-conscious practice is the process of realizing that identity matters and that it shows up in all that we do. We view situations through the lens of our own identities and experiences and then interpret those into meaning. For example, as a mother to a Black/Brown teenage boy whose friend group is also mostly Black/Brown boys, when I see a group of teenage boys hanging around on the sidewalk or in a park, what tends to be my context for them? Is my context that they could be my son and his friends enjoying some free time after a long day of school? Is my context that they are in an intense strategy session to plan out their next athletic contest or maybe even an academic decathlon? Or do I immediately think this group of Black/Brown teenage boys are up to no good? My identity as a mother to Black/Brown teenage boy has given me more context to know that this group could be doing as many (if not more) positive things than negative. For someone who only experiences or thinks of a group of Black/Brown teenage boys as troublemakers, their context for them might be that they are, indeed, up to no good. That person might call law enforcement to disperse the group. Or, if something were to happen negatively in the neighborhood (e.g., graffiti, vandalism), then maybe they assume it "must have been that group of boys" when, in fact, it also could not have been. My proximity to Black and Brown teenagers has shaped how I act, interact, and see the world around me.

Let us now take that same group of boys and place them in the classroom. When I see a group of Black/Brown teenage boys, does my context lead me to believe that they could be a group of honors and International Baccalaureate (IB) students or is my context that this group is not serious about their education and they will likely just be disengaged? My own identity and experiences and biases can shape how I approach my teaching, learning, and curriculum and my interactions with this group of students. And, as we have seen time and again, the outcomes can have a major impact.

I understand there are some people who were socialized to believe that race, color, and other identity characteristics do not matter. They grew up during a time when there was an overemphasis on "content of character, not color of skin," a misrepresented quote from Dr. Martin Luther King Jr. They were told that this quote was giving society specific directions: color doesn't matter. However, we know this to be both a misrepresentation of King's words as well as a falsehood of humanity. Identity matters. Color matters.

Race matters. While we may not like to admit that these identity markers have an impact on people's lives, experiences, and outcomes, it would be irresponsible to pretend that there is not an impact. We do not live in a post-racial society. We do not live in a class-equal society. We do not live in a society that has equal access for all. Therefore, it is important that we are conscious of the impacts of identity on our schools, communities, and lives of people so that we can reduce or mitigate these biases and build conditions where people thrive.

If you would benefit from working through some of these biases, unconscious or conscious, I recommend doing some case studies with your colleagues in the *Identity-Conscious Practice in Action* (Routledge, 2024) book. These case studies guide you in decision making through an identity-conscious lens and provide an opportunity to name, own, interrupt, and take responsibility for shaping a more inclusive community. This book can be a helpful tool as you continue to build habits and skills for this work.

Why Identity Matters in Schools

Existing research has demonstrated, in many ways, that identity shapes the teaching and learning within a community. Our schools are made up of people from different experiences, belief systems, and ideologies in addition to some of the more traditional identity categories such as race, ethnicity, language, age, disability, family structure, religion and faith traditions, and more. These identities and experiences play an influential role in the life of a school. For example, many public schools in the United States, despite being secular, schedule their academic calendar around Judeo-Christian traditions. We close our schools for "winter break," which typically privileges the celebration of Christmas. We close schools or plan "spring break" around the Easter observances. Yet our community members who observe Jewish holidays or cultural holidays (e.g., Lunar New Year) or other celebrations miss days of school or are asked to take vacation time to celebrate rather than have those holidays off. Identity matters in school because, inherently and systemically, there are already identities that experience privileges over others simply based on our school schedules.

Identity also matters when we consider the norms of our environments. Schools that require students to have types of technology in order to participate fully in school assignments yet rely on families to provide that technology on their own privilege a certain level of socioeconomic status or class. Schools that require participation in field trips or overnight events but do not consider buildings or experiences that are not accessible to an individual with mobility limitations set up privileges related to ability. Schools that consistently separate students into "boys" and "girls" and only provide restrooms, locker rooms, groups, or opportunities separated by gender privilege those who identify within a gender binary. Schools that teach only from a Eurocentric curriculum provide opportunities for White students to experience affirmation, validation, and information about who they are without expanding their understanding of other racial and ethnic perspectives, views, experiences, and ideas, thereby limiting opportunities for students from racially diverse backgrounds from learning about their history, contributions, ideas, and beliefs. Schools that hold "father-daughter" dances or "mother-son" breakfasts leave out families whose family structures are diverse and varied.

While traditions are exciting and help to build a school or grade-level identity, many traditions often leave out certain families and experiences. To make them more inclusive, try these strategies instead:

- Instead of "mother/son or father/daughter" events, host "adult/student" events.
- Instead of "guess the baby photo" (which can be problematic for students who do not have baby photos or who may have transitioned since that photo) graduation slideshow, let students select their favorite photo that celebrates who they are. If the guessing game really is essential, you can find clever ways to mask the person's identity in the photo but give enough information for people to guess.
- Instead of binary graduation clothing such as "girls wear dresses and boys wear pants," have a common color that graduates should wear, but they can choose their preferred clothing style. Alternatively, have graduation robes that cover clothing so that everyone is in a uniform outfit.
- Instead of an auction or gala that is only open to financial donors, host a community-wide event that includes opportunities to raise money without isolating people based on socioeconomic status or ability to donate.
- Instead of having employees use accrued vacation time or unpaid time off to celebrate their cultural holidays, institute a policy where employees have a certain amount of days (e.g., two days) to be used for these types of events that do not take place during scheduled school closing/vacation times.

What other "instead of . . ." scenarios occur at your school?

Time and time again, the excuse I hear is "Liza, we can't do special things for everyone." I am aware of resource constraints, population sizes, and demographics of our schools. But to pretend that identity does not matter nor that it does not impact how people experience belonging is shortsighted. To shape communities of belonging, we need to understand the impact of our decisions on different identities and be able to defend – in an equitable manner – why we make those decisions in our teaching, leading, and learning.

In thinking about the impact of identity, I often refer to the five Ps: *policies, practices, programs, procedures,* and *people.* For example, how does identity inform and impact the policies we create and uphold? How does identity inform and impact the programs we offer and to which populations? How does identity inform and impact the experiences of people in the community? In this next section, we will explore just a few examples in the five Ps that can impact teaching, learning, and curriculum.

Identity Matters in Policy: Discipline

One way in which identity shows up in schools is through the discipline process. Racial inequities, for example, in school discipline have long been of interest to school leaders, students, and families. Existing research has shown that disparities in school discipline, particularly rates between White students and Black students, continue to exist in today's schools (e.g., Gregory et al., 2010; Losen et al., 2015; Porowski et al., 2014; Smith & Harper, 2015; Vincent et al., 2011). Research examining the underlying dynamics of racial discrepancies in school discipline has uncovered a pattern of differential treatment. A national investigation of discipline referrals revealed that African American students were 3.78 times more likely to be referred to the administrative office and to receive expulsion or out of school suspension for the same or similar behavior as their White peers (Skiba et al., 2011). This is important because absence from the learning environment directly impacts academic progress.

Racial disparities in school discipline are not new but instead are a result of long-standing biases and stereotypes that are learned, reinforced, and perpetuated. These biases, often referred to as implicit biases, "are deep-seated attitudes that operate outside conscious awareness – that may even be in direct conflict with a person's stated beliefs and values" (Carter et al., 2017, p. 9). And biases do not just occur in certain parts of the country or in particular ideological spaces. Biases are everywhere. Even for schools that may espouse open-minded, diverse, and accepting views, individuals still carry early messages about race, racial groups, or racialized experiences. To address these biases, schools and communities need clear structures, protocols, and opportunities to build knowledge about biases, engage in reflection about individual biases, and create clear action plans for addressing biases and bias related incidents.

Related to teaching and learning, many disciplinary referrals occur from within the classroom. Carter et al. (2017) found that focusing on bias-free classrooms and respectful school environments was one method of reducing racial disparities in discipline. To reduce disparities, teachers and school leaders need data that is accurately disaggregated by race to determine whether different groups of students receive different penalties for the same infraction. While data matters, perception also plays a role in how students feel in the discipline process. Regardless of whether disparate disciplinary outcomes are caused by school staff racial bias, "Black students may perceive racial differences in discipline rates within their school as unfair, which in turn may have detrimental effects" (Bottiani et al., 2017, p. 2). Therefore, school leaders should start with institutional (e.g., building level, grade level, class level) data and then continue to learn about whether the perceptions of discipline vary within the school. Because racial disparities impact not only the learning environment, it is important for schools to examine the impact of bias on relationships and access to opportunities.

Evan's Story

"When I was in third grade, my teacher often singled me out for behavior. I remember so many times that this happened. There were only a few other boys of color in my predominantly white class. I honestly don't remember doing much wrong – I pretty much think my behavior was normal for an average 8-year-old boy. But, every single day, my teacher would tell me how I was misbehaving and not doing the right thing. One time, when we were lining up for recess, she pulled me out of the line and said that I couldn't join the rest of the class outside. I'm not even sure what I had done wrong. When I asked her, she said, 'You know what you did.' But honestly, I don't know. Instead of going outside to play with the rest of my class, my teacher said I had to stay inside for recess with the assistant teacher. She told me that I had to walk the long hallway where the first, second, and third grade classrooms were. She said I had to just keep walking up and down the hallway until the end of recess. When the class returned, she told me the reason I had to stay in was because I was running to line up and not walking like she said we should do. So, she kept me inside so I could practice walking. After that incident, I hated school. I asked my parents if I could go to a different school next year, one where I would not be one of the only Black/Brown boys. The next fall, I went to that new school and there were so many other Black and Brown boys

> not only in my grade but also in my class. And I never was told that I was bad or misbehaving. I'm now a junior in high school, and unfortunately, this is one of my core memories of being a student. Sometimes I wonder if my teacher even realizes how she treated me had a lasting impact on my relationship to school."

Identity Matters in Practices: Homework and Grading

Over the past decade, there have been myriad conversations about the role and purpose of homework. According to a *Washington Post* study conducted between 2018 and 2020, high schoolers reported doing an average of 2.7 hours of homework per weeknight. The National Education Association (NEA) recommends the "10 minute per grade level maximum" guidance. Essentially, 1st graders should have no more than 10 minutes of homework each night, 6th graders should have no more than 60 minutes, and 12th graders should have no more than 120 minutes each night. However, it is not just the quantity of homework but also the quality of the assignments. The NEA (2019) also reports there is only a minimal correlation between homework and academic achievement through 6th grade. Homework that is not meaningful, and instead, "busy work" has been found to increase anxiety, stress, conflict, and can impact important developmental functions like unstructured play, a routine bedtime, and family time. Yet meaningful homework can teach young people about time management, routines, and building good study habits for the future.

While research is still out about the effectiveness of homework in elementary grades, receiving homework in upper elementary grades and high school is near unavoidable, but the amount of homework has impacts at this age group. For example, the recommended amount of sleep for high schoolers is 8–10 hours of sleep, but many high schoolers actually go to bed later, often closer to 11:30 P.M. or later, due to homework and activities, resulting in chronic sleep deprivation. According to the Centers for Disease Control, chronic sleep deprivation can result in higher risk of obesity, diabetes, injuries, poor mental health, and problems with attention and behavior. Of course, homework is not the only contributor to this lack of sleep. According to the U.S. Bureau of Labor Statistics (2024), 20–23% of high school students report working a part-time job after school. According to the Armstrong-Carter (2023) report, an estimated one in five middle and high school students are also caregivers for their families. Related to identity, the same report found that these caregiving youth are mostly girls, from lower-income families, and/or hold historically marginalized racial and ethnic identities (Armstrong-Carter et al., 2022).

Over a decade ago, writer Alfie Kohn (2012) penned an essay titled "The Case Against Homework," summarizing that homework is "all pain and no gain." Yet, according to the National Center for Educational Statistics (2016), 95% of grade school children and just over 91% of high school students report they have homework. This inquiry began a movement in schools to research the role of homework and effectiveness in schools. Some school districts decided that homework was not serving the function that many believed it should serve. One group believes that homework should be a review of material from class. Others believe that students should engage in rigorous independent work so that they can demonstrate this knowledge in the upcoming class. Based on the espoused philosophy of the purpose of homework, teachers assign different types of tasks to support either review of material or an independent deep dive.

Homework is also not created equal. Given the role of identity and experiences, there has been a divide related to access and completion of homework. In a study conducted by the National Educators Association, Claire McLaughlin (2016) found that digital divide perpetuated inequities in schools across the country. She highlighted the homework gap between students in homes that do not have access to the internet and those who do. According to a recent study by three major organizations – the Hispanic Heritage Foundation, Family Online Safety Institute, and My College Options – nearly 50% of students say they have been unable to complete a homework assignment because they didn't have access to the Internet or a computer. Furthermore, 42% of students say they received a lower grade on an assignment due to lack of access.

Certainly, this inquiry is not United States specific. In a global report by Georgetown Psychology (2025), countries that give kids less homework often see better academic results than those that overload students. These practices demonstrate that educators understand a tired, stressed brain has a hard time learning and instead prioritize rest and well-being, so students come to class ready to focus and actually enjoy learning. Some worry that a reduction in homework will equal a reduction in academic achievement. However, the Georgetown study showed that Finnish, South Korean, and Japanese students spend, on average, three hours per week doing homework, and these students consistently score well in international assessments. This demonstrates that there have been places that have achieved success in reducing homework, reducing anxiety and stress, and improving test scores.

Identity Matters in Procedures: Grading

Connected to the philosophy of homework is the practice of grading and assessment. Studies have shown that grading can be heavily influenced by bias. Even before grading occurs, the types of questions that are asked on tests and assessments may be biased. One of the most contested areas of bias in assessment has been standardized testing, such as the SATs and other high-stakes tests. As Professor Ibram Kendi, author of *How to be Anti-Racist*, stated, "Standardized tests have become the most effective racist weapon ever devised to objectively degrade Black and Brown minds and legally exclude their bodies from prestigious schools."

The consequences of these standardized tests continue to perpetuate inequality through property values and schools. According to a 2019 study conducted by GreatSchools, areas with highly rated schools usually see increases in property values. Disproportionately, schools that received lower rankings were in predominantly Black and Brown neighborhoods. This cycle is significant given that public schools are supported by real estate taxes and property values, thereby continuing to privilege resources and opportunities in White, well-resourced neighborhoods.

Identity informs and impacts teacher behavior and assessment. For example, implicit biases can affect teacher behavior towards students (Rynders, 2019; Starck et al., 2020). These interactions (e.g., relationship building, engagement during class, assessment, grading of assignments) can be influenced by identity factors such as race, gender, socioeconomic background, and sexual orientation. For example, existing research has demonstrated that teacher biases can impact grading. In turn, these grades can impact a student's transcript and opportunities to engage in particular post-secondary school choices. In addition to content-based evaluations and grading, some teachers include nonacademic metrics into their grading system, such as grades for participation, "neat" binders, or rewards for turning in assignments early. While these aspects might contribute to overall skill learning related to organization, the assessment of these factors into an academic grade does not solely measure academic progress. Since we know that biases are embedded in metrics such as behavior and expectations, it is important to consider how identity, assumptions about identity, and stereotypes might be impacting grading and assessment.

Identity Matters in Programs: Tutoring and Academic Coaching Programs

When I was working at a well-resourced private school, I oversaw academic support initiatives for students in grades 6–12. This academic coaching program was designed to initially provide support for students whose families could not afford outside tutoring; therefore, the in-school tutoring was paid for by the school, and the tutoring center was staffed by content-specific faculty. Middle school students came to the center after school because they did not have after-school sports or clubs. High school students came during their free periods because many were involved in junior varsity or varsity athletics after school. When word got around that there was a space where students could go during the school day to receive free academic coaching, other families – those who could afford tutoring outside of school – wanted their children to be connected to the program. Other families chose to hire tutors to come to their homes or enroll in popular, nationally recognized tutoring organizations.

The role of socioeconomics and how this identity informed and impacted tutoring services was an important inquiry at this school. This situation forced the school and leadership team to have direct conversations about the terms "equality" and "equity." Parents who wanted their children to have access to free tutoring, regardless of whether they could pay, believed that every student should have equal access. However, equity required us to have difficult conversations about which families needed cost-free tutoring to access success.

There was another identity category that complicated the practice of offering tutoring sessions at the school: race. Students whose families could not afford outside tutoring and who accessed the academic coaching center were Black. When students, regardless of their ability to pay, accessed the academic coaching center, the program population was racially mixed. The school leadership had difficult conversations about the perceptions people might have about who came to tutoring and who needed cost-free tutoring.

These types of difficult conversations are not unique to tutoring and academic coaching spaces. There are several examples in our teaching, learning, and curriculum where we try to solve for one issue that might be impacted by identity only to discover that other aspects of identity also have an impact. It is important, as a school community, to ask ourselves the difficult and often uncomfortable questions about how our practices might be shaped by identity, which identities are included, and which identities are left out.

Identity Matters in Procedures: Bias Response Protocols

I frequently am asked to consult with a school community when an issue of bias has occurred. The most common incident is when a racial slur has been said, or offensive graffiti has been written on a bathroom wall or hallway. My first question in the consultation is always "What is your existing procedure for responding to these events?" Many times, the answer is "We just sort of take it as a case-by-case basis."

A division leader contacted me to say that a student had written a racial slur on a piece of paper and then passed that paper around to the class. A student whose identity was most impacted by that racial slur saw the paper and immediately told the teacher. The teacher demanded that someone come forward and admit they wrote the slur. Predictably, no one did. She grew frustrated and said, "Well, then none of us are going out for recess until we solve this issue." The students missed recess, and the school day ended without anyone coming forward.

What was missing from this scenario? Despite a lack of understanding that people do not always willingly and publicly admit they are responsible for something that had such a negative impact, the teacher did not do anything to address the needs of the student whose identity was most targeted. While the other students simply saw this as a "bad word written on a piece of paper," the student saw it as a threat. They saw it as a clear message that they do not belong in the class. When they saw no one taking responsibility for the note, they grew even more upset realizing their classmates would not even speak up.

In another example, a teacher was covering a unit on mental health in a psychology class. One assignment the teacher created was to set up a debate in class about "Whether people with mental health issues are more likely to commit crimes." Based on their own stereotypes, students who were assigned the affirmative – that, yes, people with mental health issues are more likely to commit crimes – cheered at how easy this debate would be. Students who were assigned the negative – that, no, people with mental health issues were not more likely to commit crimes – groaned and said how hard this was going to be. Gracie, a student in the class, was receiving ongoing outpatient treatment for mental illness and grew uncomfortable with her peers' overwhelming response to the prompts. She began to wonder if she would, in fact, end up committing crimes because she lives with a mental illness. While teachers often use the process of debate to help illustrate different viewpoints, the public nature of the debate assignment and the reaction of her classmates left Gracie feeling vulnerable. However, Gracie did not tell anyone about this because she was unsure who to go to.

Jojo, a Black student in the 11th grade, is taking an Advanced Placement (AP) literature class. The teacher did tell the students that they would be reading material that addressed difficult topics, such as race, oppression, power, privilege, and historical texts. While Jojo knew this and was excited to engage in the class, the teacher introduced a text that repeatedly used the full spelling of the N-word. One day, Jojo counted the number of times the N-word was said in a 50-minute class block and lost count somewhere after 30 times. Because the teacher was saying it so often and easily, Jojo's classmates were also using the full word in class. Whenever Jojo was getting ready to go to this class, they always felt sick, began to get a headache, and felt anxious. Jojo became preoccupied with wondering how they could skip class each day without penalty. While Jojo is a good student and well-liked, they did not want to say anything in class because a) Jojo chose this class and could probably have chosen a different Advanced Placement class; and b) Jojo really wanted a good college recommendation from the teacher and did not want to make the teacher feel self-conscious or refuse to write a letter for Jojo's college application. Throughout the semester, Jojo wished there was someone to talk to at school who could address the issue of how the book was being taught and the implications of the discussions related to the N-word.

It is important to remember that bias response protocols are not designed primarily for punishment. Rather, these protocols help communities identify where harm may be occurring and address not only the impact of the harm but also how to remedy the situation. Here is how a bias response protocol might have helped Gracie and Jojo:

Gracie's example: If Gracie did not feel comfortable speaking directly with the faculty member, a report through the bias response form could have been helpful in directing Gracie to other resources. For example, teachers often have mentors who are there to talk through difficult issues. By alerting Gracie's teacher of the situation, the mentor teacher could have worked with the faculty member to have options other than a class debate. In addition, Gracie's teacher could have the opportunity to work with an instructional coach or a counselor to find effective ways of delivering the information about mental health without unconsciously creating a negative learning environment.

Jojo's example: Because of the situation in the classroom, Jojo is being impacted emotionally and physically. By completing a bias response form, a caring adult could connect with Jojo and find ways to address the impact of what is happening in the classroom. In addition, the teacher could be given additional strategies for how to address texts that use the N-word, how to maintain historical accuracy, and how to also keep the integrity of the classroom safe for learning. Without these critical conversations, the teacher might believe that just saying "This class will address difficult topics" is all that needs to be said without addressing the impact of particular words.

While schools often pay attention to bias outside of the classroom, in social spaces, or during unstructured time, the reality is that bias happens inside the classroom and in teaching relationships too. Yet, due to worries about offending a teacher or not wanting to influence how a teacher might manage their classroom, administrators and school leaders often ignore the biases that occur in the classroom setting. Further, students are not always comfortable reporting issues of bias in the classroom, particularly when a faculty member is the cause of the harm.

While students were uncomfortable addressing issues of bias with their faculty or teachers, they did feel comfortable telling their friends or other trusted adults at school about what they experienced. However, without processes or protocols for sharing the feedback with their teachers and only informally discussing these incidents in social circles, there is little accountability for the behavior. This dynamic often contributes to the belief that experiencing bias in the classroom is just part of what happens at school.

Bias response protocols can be helpful by giving the community a specific place to articulate concerns and incidents. By having a bias response protocol in place, schools signal their awareness that identity matters and that they are taking issues related to identity seriously. And, in an environment that is committed to belonging, it is important to know when issues related to identity come up. A bias response protocol can be a helpful tool in managing incidents and addressing them in a way that reduces, not contributes to, harm.

The actual structure of a bias response protocol varies depending on the need of the school. Overall, bias response protocols give people a place to put incidents of hurt – intentional or unintentional – that they might experience in the classrooms, hallways, athletic fields, and common spaces. Focused on identity-based harm, the process allows people to be able to name what happened, provide suggestions for follow up, and begin difficult but important conversations with those who may have caused harm.

Bias response protocols are not punishments; they are not intended to be used for gossip or malice. Instead, these protocols and procedures help a community bring some of the hidden incidents – or ones that never get reported – to light so that schools can address these incidents effectively and repair harm that has been caused. If we are to assume best intent, it may be true that the teachers did not realize the impact of their actions. They may have believed that their teaching methods were effective and provided opportunities for critical thinking. However, they did not consider identity and the impact of identity. If a student was not comfortable in a 1:1 conversation with a teacher, the bias response protocol provides the teacher with a mentor or a critical friend to talk through their teaching and learning outcomes. For the students who completed a bias response form and who saw follow up occur, they each would have experienced a sense of agency by formally documenting what happened to them and seeing the school leadership take these issues seriously.

Identity Matters in People: Representation

The phrase "If you can see it, you can be it" was most attributed to tennis great Billie Jean King. She emphasized the power of role models in the lives of young people and helped them see what is possible. In my academic research, I wanted to know more about how Asian Americans and Pacific Islanders chose the field of teaching when so few of us had Asian American and Pacific Islander teachers. The participants in my study stated they chose to be on this educational journey because they believed in the purpose, the process, and the outcomes of a responsible and responsive education. When asked, "Is there anything that would have really made a difference in how you felt being in education?" The participants overwhelmingly responded, "It really would have been nice to have a teacher who looked like me."

Yes, it is possible to "not see it and be it"; however, the opportunity of having representation helps to decrease isolation, increase persistence, and help pave the way for future teachers and leaders. Representation among the teaching staff and in the school is important. And the opportunities we have to impact the experiences in the classroom through our teaching, learning, and curriculum are important. Rudine Sims Bishop (1990) uses the metaphors of windows and mirrors to demonstrate the importance of representation and reflection: *windows* are opportunities for people to learn about new ideas, experiences, and views; *mirrors* are opportunities to see oneself reflected in ways that are familiar.

Using an example of racial identity, in many of our schools in the United States, most narratives are told as single stories of who people of color are and were in this country in relationship to whiteness and to White people. In most stories, examples, and historical context, White people were the heroes, the victors, the inventors, and the scholars. Yet, counternarratives to these stories amplify the contributions and stories of people of color in this country. For example, language has shifted from referring to Africans brought to this country as "slaves" and instead using language such as "enslaved," highlighting that their origins in this country were not about an identity but rather because of action. Math is not solely situated with the Greeks but rather includes historical concepts of math from, for example, Arabic and Mayan cultures. Critical math discourse pays attention to the impacts and outputs of information. Dr. Kari Kokka's (2020) study, for example, on social justice pedagogy and critical math discourse with students from a privileged school in California found that the students "gained critical mathematics consciousness, conceptualized as improving sociopolitical understanding, developing critical civic empathy, and taking action" (p. 778). By combining curricular content, critical consciousness, and identity-based approaches, the students were learning about the context of mathematics in the larger world and in their own lives. Too often, in our U.S. education system, we have excluded these contributions outside of White and Eurocentric examples, and yet research has demonstrated that including aspects of identity across the curriculum contributes to positive critical thinking.

Identity Matters in School Environment

In addition to the five Ps (policies, practices, procedures, programs, people), identity also matters more broadly in the school context. In this section, we will explore how identity matters in two key areas: access to opportunities and sense of belonging.

Identity Matters in Access to Opportunities

Despite the current presidential administration's efforts to remove diversity, equity, and inclusion (DEI) programs from K-12, higher education, and corporate initiatives, there are still major gaps in access to educational and employment opportunities that are informed and impacted by identity. For example, multiple sources across fields report that removing diversity, equity, and inclusion programs decreased trust, workplace equity, morale, and safeguards for discrimination. It is important to dismantle the myth that diversity initiatives, in hiring, for example, simply promoted people who were not qualified and instead focused only on characteristics such as race and gender. However, these diversity initiatives were in place so that people from marginalized backgrounds were not passed over simply because they were perceived, based on race and gender, for example, to be unqualified despite significant qualifications. Diversity initiatives were never intended to, nor did, simply hire people based on race or, as opponents of DEI initiatives claimed, "reverse racism."

Identity-conscious practices matter because our systems of employment, education, laws, and operations privilege the identities of those with systemic power – White, male, able-bodied, Christian, English-speaking – as the ideal worker or the norm, while positioning anyone outside of those identities as the other. Operating with an awareness of how identity informs and impacts our decisions related to employment, education, advising, and decision making allows us to consider the whole human and human experience rather than simply make judgments based on limited categories rooted in stereotypes. This is why programs designed to focus on identities have widened access. Programs like "Girls Who Code" or "Black Student Orientation" or "LGBTQ Affinity Spaces" create opportunities for people with marginalized identities to access the same opportunities as those who are White, male, able-bodied, Christian, English-speaking, etc.

The current political and social climate has impacted access to opportunities, particularly for those who hold marginalized identities. Current court rulings highlight hypocrisy in opportunities. For example, multiple court rulings have impacted initiatives known as "affinity groups," or gatherings of people who share similar identity characteristics. These groups might be race-based (e.g., Black Student union, student of color dialogue group, affinity groups) or provide targeted outreach to historically underrepresented groups (e.g., Native Science Program, Women's Leadership Initiative). Recent rulings have claimed that these opportunities privilege marginalized groups over White groups. Yet, affiinty spaces simply give access to agency that has been historically and presently missing in our current social and cultural landscape.

Despite efforts to challenge affinity spaces, the social and political climate shows its hypocrisy by pushing back against mixed groups, for example, when it comes to athletics. It is as if people do not want single-identity spaces until it infringes on their own ideologies. For example, informed by transphobia, these same groups that are interested in dismantling single-identity groups for specific people are also very passionate about making sure that "only girls should play on sports teams with girls," or more specifically, "transgender girls cannot be allowed to play nor compete with cisgender girls." This type of selective outrage contributes to the gatekeeping of opportunities.

Identity Matters to Sense of Belonging

It is generally understood that the definition of belonging includes multiple dimensions of psychological, emotional, physical, intellectual, spiritual, and social connectedness. Researchers who study belonging have described the concept as a result of "where psychological and safety needs are gratified" (e.g., Maslow, 1962). Others have described belonging as "feelings of connectedness, that one is important or matters to others" (Rosenberg & McCullough, 1981). Others have conceptualized belonging as the absence of factors such as the absence of rejection, the absence of isolation and loneliness, or the absence of marginality (e.g., Hagerty et al., 2002). In search of a working definition, Strayhorn (2018) states "sense of belonging refers to students' perceived social support, a feeling or sensation of connectedness, and the evidence of mattering or feeling cared about, accepted, respected, valued by, and important to the campus community" (p. 4). Key to this definition is the reciprocity of the relationship – that each member benefits from the group and each group benefits from the contributions of its members through shared commitments.

While belonging is important to every student, Murphy and Zirkel (2015) argue that "the nature and meaning of belonging in school is different for students targeted by negative racial stereotypes – such as African American, Latino/a, Native American, and some Asian American students" (p. 3). Because of the racialized nature of belonging, it is important for schools to understand how different racialized groups are impacted by belonging, as studies have revealed that a positive sense of belonging can impact academic engagement, motivation and persistence, and academic achievement.

As demonstrated in this book, belonging can be an outcome of effective teaching, intentional learning environments, and a responsive curriculum. Using an identity-conscious lens, teachers and school leaders can implement activities, processes, and assessments that include different identities – both present and absent from the class or community – as ways to provide the windows and mirrors that Bishop (1990) identified as being important contributors.

The Deficit Lens and Identity

While an identity-conscious practice focuses on the ways in which identity can be used to center an asset-based approach to teaching, learning, and curriculum development, early research into identity often addressed this from a deficit lens or how negative experiences are a result of identity. In my own teaching practice, there have been several times when I assigned articles to my class, only to realize during the class discussion that the readings I chose were from a deficit lens.

Because this work is ongoing, it means we might still make mistakes. One semester, I had several students who identified as gender non-binary and gender fluid. I intentionally searched for articles that addressed the experiences of gender non-binary and gender fluid students and even took the extra effort to make sure those articles were written or at least coauthored by a researcher who held those same identities. I thought I had done a very inclusive thing. However, it was clear that I had chosen research articles focused on negative experiences of gender non-binary and gender fluid students. In an effort to be inclusive by adding readings that include issues of gender and gender spectrum, I instead created a very negative learning environment not only for the students who identified as gender non-binary and gender fluid but also for the students who did not identify in these ways; they, too, were now reading deficit-focused articles about this community.

So what did I do? We continued with discussing the readings. I felt uncomfortable. And, despite having the teaching skills to navigate this, my emotional insecurity got the best of me. *I froze.* The students had journal entries due that evening, and every student addressed how uncomfortable it was to be in class earlier that day and how there was such misalignment with what they believed I wanted to do as a teacher and what happened. While email was not ideal, I reached out individually to the few students who openly identified as gender non-binary and gender fluid and accepted responsibility for my failure in class, for the impact that my choices had, and for the learning environment I had created. I then sent a note to the entire class naming what had occurred, owning my mistake, and taking responsibility for not only the articles I assigned but also for my failure to admit what had gone wrong in real time. I then let them know my follow-up actions would be to remove those readings from the required list (and offered them as optional readings so they could continue to gain exposure to researchers from diverse identities). The next time I taught the class, I was more responsible in making sure the articles I chose included gender non-binary and gender fluid students from an asset-based lens.

The choices we make are not neutral. When I take ownership for my actions, I understand that my own use of those articles was rooted in the lack of knowledge and experience I had with gender non-binary and gender fluid students in the classroom. I understand that my limited scope of research kept these identities at a distance from my own awareness. And, as the faculty member responsible for creating my curriculum, I continue to interrogate how my own identities informed not only how I taught but also how I evaluated what went into the curriculum.

Institutional Impacts of a Deficit-Only Lens

A deficit lens is often examining the experiences and outcomes of students through the prism of their shortcomings. It tends to focus on individual responsibility and actions and de-emphasizes the role of institutional policies and practices that are informed by racism, classism, sexism, and other oppressive structures. In this deficit lens, educators tend to believe in the meritocracy principles that espouse "if people just worked hard(er), they would achieve more." The deficit lens model is most harmful to students who come from different marginalized identities such as high-poverty communities, Black and Brown students, first-generation students, and English language learners. Teachers who hold biases – conscious or unconscious – against these communities tend to demonstrate classroom behaviors such as lower expectations, decentering of community cultural wealth, and limiting exposure to a rigorous curriculum.

There have been efforts made to counteract the impact of a deficit lens. Suneal Kolluri and Antar Tichavakunda (2023) examined a counter-deficit approach to research and education to challenge racism in schools and improve opportunities for marginalized youth. However, in their research, they discovered that though educators understood that racism was both an ideological and a structural force, many continued to address racism as *only* an ideological problem and failed to address racism as a *structural* issue. In addition to changing hearts and minds, a common approach to diversity work, we need to address the root causes of underachievement and failure and not just the individual complexities of factors such as socioeconomic status, racial and ethnic backgrounds, and family structures (Garcia & Guerra, 2004).

Working closely with schools, I have seen the lack of interrogation related to institutional policies, practices, programs, and procedures that contribute to low achievement and failure. Having worked closely with teachers, I understand the frustration that comes with seeing low achievement and failure results for students. Some teachers respond with "There is only so much time in the day. And I have so many students. I'm doing the best that I can." Others respond with "This is just the way it is. We have tried everything. We can't change society, racism, and their conditions." There is a real resignation occurring in some of our schools and among some of our educators that just see this current educational-political-social climate as destined to be what it is: failing our students.

So what are the remedies to this approach? Is it even possible to shift climate and culture without falling into the trap that Zaretta Hammond (2025) calls "PD'ing our way out of inequity"? Garcia and Guerra (2004), along with other researchers, offer a few suggestions:

- Rather than focus on teacher improvement, focus on elements of institutional culture that lead to marginalizing or reinforcing inequity.
- Focus on school culture that might privilege or favor some students over others. While we all hold individual biases, some of these biases are reinforced in our institutional culture. Identify these and begin to interrupt or disrupt inequitable practices.
- Using an identity-conscious lens, build skills in both White teachers and teachers of color to identify how other aspects of their identities might be contributing to a deficit lens approach institutionally. For example, though a teacher of color might connect well with Black

and Brown students, it is possible that the teacher also holds biases related to socioeconomic status, language, ability, and gender that are impacting a deficit lens approach. Provide opportunities for deep and meaningful reflection that can be turned into action in teaching, learning, and curricular practices.

Taken together, these three examples help us to shift from solely focusing on the individual habits and skills of teachers but holding the institution accountable for the ways in which these deficit lenses are perpetuated.

Identity-Conscious Theories

An important component of an identity-conscious approach is to be critical of what we know, what we believe, and what we do. Therefore, in addition to the practice of identity-conscious reflection, it is important that we also lean on theories that can shape how we make choices in our teaching, learning, and curriculum. In this section, we will explore a few critical frameworks to situate identity and apply an identity-positive lens.

Before we even get into the different theories, however, let us do this thing – talk about how these frameworks took on a life of their own in the mid-2020s. I want to make sure you have the opportunity to think about the ongoing climate around issues related to race, identity, and education before we even get into how to address our practices from an identity-conscious lens. So let us explore a bit about what went down in the mainstream media.

Media's Hype of Theoretical Frameworks

"But do you teach CRT?" – a question many K-12 educators had to answer in the mid-2020s.

"I'll answer that question after you accurately define for me what C-R-T is." – every exhausted teacher

In the mid-2020s, it seemed as if everyone I ran into "knew" what critical race theory (CRT) was. Yet I was constantly amazed at how misunderstood and misrepresented one of the most important theoretical frameworks to the field of education was manipulated to stoke fear, anxiety, and anger. The combination of ignorance and intentional misleading fueled the fire in educational spaces.

For a few months, it seemed every news source, school committee meeting, and parent-teacher conference was filled with opinions about critical race theory. When I asked parents and caregivers what their anti-CRT stance was, many responded with "You're teaching children that they are racist!" or "You're making them feel bad for things they didn't even do!" or "You're teaching them things that are too mature for them to understand!" First of all, no. Every responsible educator who has training, practice, and skill in teaching does so in age-appropriate ways. No, kindergarten students were forgoing learning how to write the alphabet and stopped at the letters "C-R-T" (I swear, someone said this to me). No, kindergarten students were not being forced to accept responsibility for enslavement, oppressive policy creation, and the upholding of inequitable treatment in society. No, middle school White students were not being forced to give up their spots in clubs and organizations for less-qualified students of color. And no, affirmative action was not reverse racism against White candidates.

But a few minutes of watching the 24-hour news cycle, we certainly were led to believe that critical race theory was all the rage in K-12 education. Suddenly, teachers were "indoctrinators" and pushing an agenda. And yet, with the exception perhaps of children from activist families, no K-12 students could tell me who Kimberle Crenshaw nor Derrick Bell are (two foundational contributors to critical race theory). School committees began to hold hearings on whether schools should be teaching CRT (again, schools were not teaching CRT) and what the penalties should be for those caught teaching CRT.

The Department of Education issued a "Dear Colleague" letter in February 2025, stating schools needed to sign a verification statement that they were not teaching "D-E-I," and if so, they would have funding pulled from their programs. In August 2025, the justice department stated that requiring people to sign such statements would violate the first amendment for free speech. And, in January 2026, the Department of Education dropped their appeal.

To be clear, teaching about CRT is different from teaching about race. Critical race theory (CRT) is a legal framework used to interrogate laws and policies. It was then adapted by educational scholars to examine how educational systems (e.g., laws, policies) upheld inequity based on race. And yet the fearmongering of CRT soon translated to "Schools cannot teach anything about race." Also, side note, *not* teaching about race *is* teaching about race. How? Because not teaching about different racialized experiences is teaching about whiteness. Whiteness then becomes the lens through which all of these supposedly "race neutral" lessons are being taught. Do you want to know how I know that? I know that because I applied a critical race theoretical lens to the issue of teaching and determined that not teaching about race *is* teaching about race. See how that works?

Why did we need to go through those paragraphs earlier? It is because we are about to read about critical race theory as a lens through which we can view issues of education – particularly how identity informs and impacts the educational environment. I wanted you to take a moment to think about how this has been situated in the current culture and climate of our educational landscape. If you heard about critical race theory from media pundits, I wanted to acknowledge what you might have heard, felt, and digested. And, as we continue to explore how theory and practice guide good teaching, learning, and curriculum, it was important to at least name and own what happened so we can interrupt the myths and mistakes made in the mid-2020s.

Critical Race Theory

Now that we got some of the misconceptions about critical race theory out of the way, let us do a quick primer on what critical race theory is. In this section, we will look briefly at the historical roots of critical race theory, learn the key tenets of the framework, and explore how it is used in education. From there, we can apply critical race theory as a lens through which we view teaching, learning, and curriculum.

Though the Civil Rights Acts passed in the mid-1960s, race scholars understood that these legal changes were not without critique. Scholars throughout the mid-1960s, 1970s, and 1980s framed critical legal studies to interrogate the inequities that still existed despite legal change. Critical race theory provides a lens to examine the racialized experiences of students in schools by examining the relationships among race, racism, and power. CRT has its roots in legal studies (Crenshaw, 1995), and many educational scholars have adapted and applied CRT to understand issues of school discipline, culture, climate, and processes. While change is long overdue, Ladson-Billings (1998) warns that critical race theory in education is often engaged at a slow pace and writes:

> if we are serious about solving problems (of race, racism and social justice) in our schools and classrooms, we have to be serious about intense study and careful rethinking of race and education. Adopting and adapting CRT as a framework for educational equity means we have to expose racism in education and propose radical solutions for addressing it. We will have to take bold and sometimes unpopular positions. . . . We will have to adopt a position of consistently swimming against the current. . . . But I fear we (educational researchers) may never assume the liminal position because of its dangers, its discomfort, and because we insist on thinking of ourselves as permanent residents in a nice field like education.
>
> (p. 22)

Despite inaccurate representation, which sparked ongoing political controversy surrounding critical race theory (CRT) that emerged in the early 2020s, the goals of the framework were to be a lens through which systems were examined. The following are the original tenets as described by Crenshaw (1988):

- racism is endemic to American culture;
- rejection of dominant narratives, processes, or systems that claim race neutrality, color blindness, and meritocracy;
- racism has deeply rooted origins that attribute White people with dominant status and non-White people with subordinate status;
- the voices and lived experiences of people of color are legitimate and used to generate oppositional discourses;
- recognition of interest convergence, which describes the conditions by which racial justice will be accommodated in a White power structure; and
- racism's eradication is tied to eliminating all forms of oppression.

While used as a lens to examine racial inequality through the legal landscape, the framework of CRT in education was developed to examine how race informed and impacted educational systems (Solórzano & Yosso, 2002). Based on the educational application of CRT, the following tenets were put forward:

- the predominance of curriculum that excludes the history and lived experiences of Americans of color and imposes a dominant White narrative of history;
- deficit-oriented instruction that characterizes students of color as in need of remediation;
- narrow assessments, the results of which are used to confirm narratives about the ineducability of children of color;
- school discipline policies that disproportionately impact students of color and compromise their educational outcomes (such as dress code policies prohibiting natural Black hairstyles);
- school funding inequities, including the persistent underfunding of property-poor districts, many of which are composed primarily of children of color; and
- the persistence of racially segregated education.

Taken together, critical race theory, both broadly and in education, provides a guide for assessing (though an action-based rubric) the extent of identity-conscious practices in teaching, learning, and curriculum while also recognizing the inherent power structures within education.

Embedded within the critical race umbrella are also a number of racial and ethnic frameworks, such as AsianCrit, LatCrit, NativeCrit, and MultiracialCrit. There are also critical frameworks for research, such as QuantCrit Analysis. At the root of these different frameworks is the opportunity to examine how dominant narratives are formed, perpetuated, and used to disrupt hegemonic ways of knowing. I recommend several scholars and readings that address these different ways of knowing in the pullout box.

Here are a few examples of how critical race theory inspired other critical frameworks examining identity:

DisCrit: Annamma et al. (2013) describe DisCrit (disability critical race theory) as a dual analysis of race and ability and examines the ways in which students are both raced and dis/abled.

ClassCrit: Mutua (2008) describes ClassCrit as a critical lens for examining the use and misuse of economic power and its relationship to other economic formations in society.

Critical Feminist Theory: Wood (2008) describes critical feminist theory as an umbrella term for theories used to identify, question, and seek to reform patriarchal ideologies that give rise to asymmetrical rights, opportunities, roles, and material circumstances.

LatCrit: Among a series of ethnocentric critical race theories, Iglesias (1997) explored a contextualized analysis of the cultural, political, and economic dimensions of White supremacy, particularly as it impacts Latinas/os in their individual and collective struggles for self-understanding and social justice.

AsianCrit: Museus and Iftikar (2013) describe AsianCrit as a conceptual lens for examining the ways in which race and racism can shape the lives of Asian Americans in society, the racial realities of Asian Americans, and the racialized experiences of Asian Americans.

The Importance of Building an Identity-Conscious Practice

As we examine policies, procedures, practices, programs, and traditions through a critical lens, we begin to see how an identity-conscious practice emerges. Through this approach, we see how it helps us realize that who we are informs and impacts how we act, interact, and how we see the world around us (Talusan, 2022). Rather than approach the world as identity-neutral (e.g., race neutral, class neutral, color neutral), this lens requires us to see the impact of identity. When we build an identity-conscious practice, we are choosing to see the broader spectrum of humanity, of personhood, and of how people experience the world.

Notice the order of the words in *identity-conscious-practice*. Those words and the order of the words are intentional. Identity refers to the makeup of who we are and the different experiences that we have. *Conscious* refers to the awareness that comes from reflective practice to understand who we are. *Practice* means what we do and how we demonstrate what we know and what we have learned.

Building an identity-conscious practice can occur in three steps: 1) build knowledge, 2) engage in reflection, and 3) move to action. When we *build knowledge*, we are examining the facts, reading theories, learning theoretical and conceptual frameworks to the field, and gathering information about our own environment and community. When we *engage in reflection*, we ask ourselves, "What does this information have to do with me?" We personalize the data and facts and shape relevancy to our own lives. This may mean, "What does this have to do with the grade level that I teach?" or "What does this have to do with math and science?" or "What does this have to do with how I engage students?" All of these are reflective questions that can help build our own identity-consciousness. Once we have gathered information and reflected on its relevancy to our own lives, we must then *create action* to demonstrate an identity-conscious practice.

Through this journey of building an identity-conscious practice, it is important that we build both the skills and the habits for approaching our work with teaching, learning, and curriculum. Skill-building gives us the tools to be able to name, own, and interrupt when identity-neutral approaches occur in our educational context. The habits that we build support ongoing work, ongoing reflection, and consistent commitment to action. Together, building skills and engaging in habits that are long-lasting will help transform our teaching, learning, and curriculum.

Recently, I asked my students why we should spend so much time building an identity-conscious practice in a class called "teaching, learning, and curriculum." I admit, I was a little disappointed when they did not all jump out of their seats and clamor to answer the question. In fact, I looked around at a sea of faces avoiding eye contact with me. I counted to 30 while slowly looking at each student (who were still avoiding eye contact with me). And then, I simply asked, "What is getting in the way of you answering this question?" One courageous student replied, "I have just never thought of how these three separate things – teaching, learning, and curriculum – could be shaped by identity. So I'm struggling to connect the dots, even though I know the dots are there." "Fair enough," I responded.

Next, I scaffolded the dialogue in this way:

First, we are made up of many different identities.
Second, our identities are shaped by what we have experienced, what our cultures tell us, who we know, what we know, and what we believe to be true.
Third, teaching, learning, and curriculum are not neutral. They are shaped by people who have been influenced by their own lives and experiences.
Fourth, those people who are influencing the work hold identities that shape what we teach, learn, and include in our curriculum
Fifth, and therefore, an identity-conscious practice helps us to unmask and reveal how identity is influencing our teaching, leading, and learning so that we can boost things that create greater access and equity for all and reduce biases that may be impacting success.

"I mean, that makes sense," replied one of the students.

"Well, there will be more where that came from," I responded.

Each of the activities you see at the end of the sections are ones that I facilitate with my students. These activities have helped them to name, own, and interrupt actions that get in the way of access and equity. These biases and blank spots might get in the way of building relationships, fostering an inclusive environment, and even keeping students from fully engaging in learning activities.

The activities in the next section are designed to help you begin the process of building an identity-conscious practice. These activities serve as the foundation for the work we will be doing and can serve as a helpful touchpoint when you are shaping lessons, developing activities, and assessing learning outcomes.

Activities for Building an Identity-Conscious Practice

In this previous section, you had the opportunity to build knowledge and engage in reflection about how identity may have shaped your own approach to teaching, learning, and curriculum. Individually, complete these activities. If you have peer learning communities or colleagues to engage in dialogue or work, there are discussion questions at the end of this section that can further your learning.

Activity 1: 5-Minute Writing Prompts

As a way to build community in a peer learning group, these 5-minute writing prompts are helpful ways to engage in reflection about teaching. These prompts can be used 1) solely as a reflective exercise in a journal, 2) a think-write-pair-share, and/or 3) a large group share-out.

Prompt #1: Describe an activity (e.g., sport, instrument, dance) that you had to engage in practice. What do you remember about those practices? How did you feel in those practices? When did you tend to get frustrated? When did you tend to feel joy/celebration in those practices? How might identity have informed and impacted this experience?

Prompt #2: Choose one of your grade/class levels from your past (e.g., 3rd grade, 10th-grade chemistry class). Describe as many aspects of the classroom, people, and environment as possible. Be descriptive about identity and utilize your senses to create a picture of this memory. What feelings emerge because of thinking about this prompt?

Prompt #3: What identities have been most represented in your family life? In your social life? In your professional life? What, if any, has been the impact of this representation in these spaces?

Prompt #4: How would you describe "identity" to these different age levels? What is different about how you are explaining it to these different age levels? What informed your choice to do it this way?

1) To a 5-year-old
2) To a 16-year-old
3) To a peer
4) To someone significantly older than you

Activity 2: Proximity

Proximity is a way to understand our "closeness" or "distance" to certain identities and experiences. In this exercise, there is a thorough – yet incomplete – list of identities and experiences that we might hold and/or encounter in our work. Using the columns to the right, identify the position of these identities and experiences based on your "closeness" or "distance" to them.

Some categories may be listed as large groups. You are welcome to identify subgroups or experiences within that larger category if that works best for your chart (e.g., "race" can be divided into subgroups such as "Black, Asian, Native American, Latino/a/e, White, Multiracial").

Core = This identity is very close to who you are; it's an identity that shapes how you move through the world, who you are at your core, and how you see the world around you. This importance stays relatively stable and does not change.

Important but Distance = This identity tends to be one that is important to you, but its importance changes based on context. Maybe it is more important depending on where you go or who you are with, and therefore, its meaning and impact might change depending on the environment.

Unfamiliar = This identity tends to be one that you do not often think about unless you are reminded of it – or perhaps do not think about at all. You move through the world not really paying much attention to this nor can understand this from a personal perspective. While it may be important to someone else, its level of importance in your own life signals a weak connection to it.

Identity/Experience (you may also use the additional space to be more specific within the category	**Core (very close, very familiar)**	**Important (aware but some distance)**	**Unfamiliar (furthest from your own experiences)**
E.g., Race *Asian* *Black* *Latino/a/e* *Native Indigenous* *White* *Multiracial*	*X (very close to my experience)*	*X (my husband and children are Black/Latine, but I am not)*	*X (I do not have any close experiences as Native/Indigenous)* *X (I am not White and do not know what this experience would be like)*
Class Wealthiest class Upper middle Middle Working Poverty (others)			
Race Asian Black/African Latina/o/e Native/Indigenous White Multiracial (others)			

Identity/Experience (you may also use the additional space to be more specific within the category	**Core (very close, very familiar)**	**Important (aware but some distance)**	**Unfamiliar (furthest from your own experiences)**
Sex Male Female Non-Binary Transgender (others)			
Sexual Orientation Heterosexual Lesbian Gay Bisexual (others)			
Religious/Faith Christian Catholic Evangelical Hindu Jewish Muslim Atheist (others) **Add additional categories in these boxes**			

Activity 3: Consciousness

Select two to three of the categories listed earlier. To practice reflection, please respond to the following prompts:

1) Please select one of the aforementioned categories you would like to focus on for this activity (e.g., race, gender, class, religion).
2) As you reflect on that category or subcategory, what moments or experiences come to mind that spark a memory for you?
3) What are you conscious of when you think about that category or subcategory? Where does that consciousness come from?
4) What do you notice you might be unconscious or unaware of? Where does that unconsciousness or unawareness come from?
5) How did you feel filling out the chart earlier and engaging in this reflection about consciousness raising?

Activity 4: Practice – Start, Stop, Change, Continue

In an identity-conscious practice, we build knowledge, engage in reflection, and move to action. As you consider your teaching, learning, curriculum, and identity, what are some action items you can start doing; stop doing; change or edit just a bit; or continue doing in order to build an identity-conscious practice?

Category	What I Can Start Doing	What I Can Stop Doing	What I Can Change/Edit	What I Can Continue Doing
Asian American students	*I can do an assessment of where in my curriculum there are stories, images, or experiences of Asian Americans.*	*I can stop leaving out Asian American stories and be more aware of how little they are represented.*	*We are already doing morning read-aloud, so I can add an Asian American text or story or highlight someone in this morning share.*	*I believe I do a good job connecting with Asian American students and families, so I'm going to continue reaching out and being intentional about making sure they belong.*
Add your categories or subcategories here				

Part I Discussion Questions

With a peer learning group, discuss the following questions:

1. An identity-conscious practice is three parts: identity + conscious + practice. What did you experience as you looked at the many different identities and experiences that could shape our world and our work?
2. What did you experience as you raised your level of consciousness or awareness about certain identities in your life? What a-ha moments might you have experienced as you looked back at your chart/consciousness exercise?
3. Based on your observation of identity and this consciousness raising, what action items come to mind? What, if anything, are you compelled to explore or do as a result of this work?
4. What application of an identity-conscious practice do you anticipate in teaching, learning, and curriculum?
5. In this section, you may have learned some new terms, theories, frameworks, and concepts. What, in this section, is a concept you would like to learn more about? What would be different about your teaching, learning, and/or curriculum if you knew more about that concept?

Part II

Identity-Conscious Teaching

Key elements

- What does the research say about teacher identity and pedagogy?
- What are some key contributions to the field of teaching and identity?
- What does it mean to decolonize our teaching practices?
- What theories help us understand teaching through an identity-conscious lens?
- How does bias and anti-bias approaches to teaching show up?

Introduction

I fall into the large category of people who have wanted to teach ever since they were young. I made my two younger siblings go through "class time" during summer vacations, drawing numbers and letters on the chalkboard that my dad had installed in our family room. I sought out opportunities to teach karate class as a teenager, summer academic camp in my early college years, and workshops as a graduate teaching assistant. I had opportunities to serve as a dean of faculty in a summer program, a program focused on supporting prospective teachers in the field. I was mentored by classroom teachers and learned how to effectively plan lessons, address behavior, and teach in a student-centered way. I learned how to be responsive in the classroom, read the emotional temperature in the room, and observe not only

DOI: 10.4324/9781003784739-3

verbal answers but also physical body language that communicated whether a student was present. I took advantage of many professional development opportunities, workshops, and peer learning groups to improve my teaching. In adulthood, I enrolled in a coaching certification program so that I could better guide adults in their practice of teaching.

Along the way, I engaged in deep reflection about teaching, specifically, "How did I get into teaching when my own learning experiences left me without role models?" I did not learn about my own identity as an Asian American in the K-12 curriculum, and I did not have any teachers who identified as Asian American. How could I "be" it when I have never "seen it"? In fact, the first Asian American/Pacific Islander professor I had was when I enrolled in my doctoral program. I went through K-12, undergraduate, master's program, and many professional development workshops without any Asian American teachers, leaders, professors, or facilitators.

During my sophomore year in college, I had the opportunity to learn from a multiracial/Black professor named Dr. Michelle Dunlap. Dr. Dunlap was early in her career when I met her in 1994. She was energetic, kind, and eager to be in community with students. She taught classes in psychology and child development and often used her own experiences to bring the course content to life. While most of my high school teachers maintained a level of distance, I remember feeling so connected to Professor Dunlap. While I did love the subject matter and ended up minoring in child development (now human development), I really went to class because I wanted to be around her. For the first time in my educational life, I felt seen by a teacher. I saw myself reflected in her lessons. I continued to take classes with her as she taught about multicultural communities. Her teaching about people, cultures, and educational practices were not rooted in whiteness. When I wrote papers, she always gave critical feedback in a way that made me feel challenged and supported. She was the first person to introduce me not only to the concept but to the implementation of what we now call trauma-informed teaching because she always thought of how we, as students, were receiving information. To this day, over 30 years since I graduated from college, whenever I see Professor Dunlap, I become overwhelmed with gratitude. *Okay, let me put it plainly – I cry.* Whenever I see her, her very presence reminds me of why I wanted to not just teach but to also be *great* at teaching. I did not realize it before meeting her, but she was the teacher that my younger self was waiting for.

The impact of her teaching is so evident in my own. I strive to know each of my students – not just who they are in front of me in class but also what motivates them, what inspires them, and what led them to education. I want to know them well enough to be able to see them in class and know something is not quite right. And, on those days, I want to approach them with kindness, compassion, and gratitude for learning that day. I want to know about my students so that I can change, shape, and adjust my curriculum to be more reflective of who they are, ideally challenging their sense of self and of the world. I want to share parts of who I am in service of teaching, connecting, and learning. I strive to give feedback that is both critical and rooted in care for my students. I want them to know that my attention to them is informed by respect, especially when we are in conflict. I want them to know that, yes, what we are doing is difficult and sometimes feels impossible and that they are worth the struggle.

In my 30 years in education, I did not spend all of it as a good teacher. Early in my career, I was not confident in my own abilities and even some of the content, and my teaching was largely sterile and robotic. I just felt like "I need to get through this content" and did not know the difference between "learning" and "engagement." Instead, I measured success by whether we finished a unit on time, not how the students experienced the class. I struggled to build relationships, to build trust, and to have students enjoy learning. While I loved teaching, my inexperience showed in the evaluations. Students reported that there was simply too much focus on content and not enough time to think, reflect, apply, and practice. When I read these evaluations, I was insecure and often asked myself, "What am I even doing as a teacher?" I knew I had two choices: get better or leave the field.

I chose to get better.

The Landscape of Teaching

Whether it involved teaching early hunters-gatherers, religious clergy, agricultural practices, mechanical skills, literature and the arts, or role-specific knowledge, teaching has been an essential part of information production. According to the Public Broadcasting System's "Only a Teacher" series, during the mid-to-late 1700s, teaching was not a formal profession. Rather, teaching positions were held by those who were using teaching as a stepping stone to a career in law or the church. In the mid-1800s, school reformers such as Horace Mann wanted to shape schools to be more democratic, universal, and nonsectarian, creating the first public school or Common School.

Until the middle of the nineteenth century, most formal school learning was taking place in one-room schools and led by a male teacher. In the mid-1800s, the Common Schools hired women to teach. Soon, Normal Schools that provided training for teachers were established. Their goal was to prepare teachers for the growing needs of the Common Schools. By the turn of the twentieth century, nearly 75% of America's teachers were women (PBS, 2001).

Though there have been ideological and practical changes to the field of teaching since its formal beginning, teaching tends to be approached in two important ways: the science of teaching and the art of teaching. While the science of teaching tends to refer to the use of research-based strategies for instruction, the art of teaching tends to refer to a teacher's professional judgment and experience in knowing what to use with individual students. In the text *What Works in Schools*, Robert Marzano (2003) presents three general characteristics of effective teaching: 1) use of effective instructional strategies, 2) use of effective classroom management strategies, and 3) use of effective curriculum design.

While many books on the art and science of teaching provide robust strategies on learning outcomes, activities, and assessment, few discuss the implications of identity in the teaching practice. In my work on identity-conscious practices, I encourage educators to consider the role of identity and how it informs and impacts our approaches to teaching. As we continue our work together in this book, it is important to understand the particular social, economic, and political barriers that restricted access to teaching and perpetuated a lack of racial diversity in the profession – effects that are still felt today.

White Women Teaching

Recent professional data in the field of education demonstrates that White women predominantly make up the demographics of teachers in the United States. From an identity-conscious lens, the teaching profession in the United States is predominantly White and female due to historical, economic, and structural factors, including systemic hiring discrimination after desegregation and current systemic inequities in teacher preparation programs. According to the National Center for Education Statistics, about three quarters (77%) of teachers are women, and the gender balance is especially significant in elementary schools, where 89% of teachers are women. In addition, 80% of public school elementary and secondary school teachers identified as non-Hispanic White, 9% identified as Hispanic, 6% identified as Black, 2% identified as Asian American, 2% identified as multiracial, and fewer than 1% identified as Pacific Islander or American Indian and Native Alaskan (NCES, 2021).

Why is it significant to explore these teacher statistics through an identity-conscious lens? Existing published research on teaching has confirmed that teachers of color improve outcomes for students of color, likely due to higher expectations, cultural alignment, proximity, and fewer biased-related disciplinary actions. According to the National Council on Teacher Quality (2023),

Black teachers (and teachers of color in general) have a well-documented positive impact on Black students' academic lives and outcomes. Researcher David Blazar (2024) in his article "Why We Need More Black Teachers" found that assignment to a Black teacher, for example, had positive impacts on students' social emotional learning, attendance, and test scores. In addition, Blazar (2024) found that teachers of color were more likely than White teachers to build interpersonal relationships with students and families, to spend more time differentiating instruction, and to move past a fixed mindset in student learning.

This is not to overgeneralize teachers of color. I distinctly remember a parent-teacher conference I attended when I encountered such a moment. My child's teacher was a Black woman with decades of teaching experience. My husband and I were excited to meet her, as our child had few Black teachers at their predominantly Black high school. When we sat down, her first words were "I didn't realize (xxxx) was smart!" My husband and I both looked at each other. "I'm sorry, what did you say?" I asked. She replied, "I didn't know (xxxx) was smart. I just assumed he was just another teenager in my class. But (xxxx) has been asking good questions, and I thought to myself, 'I guess (xxxx) is smart!'" My husband and I remained confused for the remainder of the 20-minute conference. Several times during the meeting, we said, "Yes, (xxxx) is smart. He is a hard worker, intelligent, responsible, and very serious about his future." We tried to give the teacher a chance to recover from what we felt was a very biased-informed relationship with our child, but she never quite caught on. She just kept repeating, "I just can't believe that (xxxx) is smart! (xxxx) just didn't seem like he'd be smart." Unfortunately, our child often reported throughout the school year that this was his least favorite class, that he never connected with this teacher, and that this was no longer a subject of interest.

So, yes, of course, there are exceptions to the research that has found that teachers of color tend to raise expectations for students of color, build stronger relationships, and engage in differentiated instruction more than White teachers. But overwhelmingly, the research continues to point out how important it is for students of color, in particular, to engage with teachers of color.

The Impact of Brown vs Board of Education: Racial Changes in the Teaching Force

Why are most of the teachers White? When, historically and systemically, did we see the change in racial demographics of teachers? Landmark educational cases such as *Brown v Board of Education*, one of the nation's most significant milestones for civil rights, contributed to the decline of Black educators employed by schools. The outcome of *Brown v Board* afforded Black children the same educational opportunities as White children and ended the practice of "separate but equal." However, it also contributed to the forced resignation of Black teachers in Black-only schools. As a result of the Supreme Court decision and the implementation of desegregation, tens of thousands of Black educators and principals lost their jobs as White educators and leaders refused to hire Black teachers over White teachers. These created threats to the economic, social, and cultural structure of the Black community (Tillman, 2004) impacted by the of loss of Black educators.

As Linda Tillman (2004) writes in the historical perspective of *Brown v Board of Education*:

> A tradition of Black excellence and education dates back to the 1860s. Black educators helped to build and operate schools, secure funding and other needed resources, worked with the Black community, and worked as advocates for the education of Black children. In addition, the educational philosophies of Black educators generally reflected the collective ethos of a Black community that believed education was the key to enhancing the life chances of their children.
>
> (p. 282)

Tillman writes that the impact of desegregation was devastating to Black teachers and principals. Black teachers were deemed to be inferior educators to Whites and were not hired to teach in desegregated schools. Some school boards demanded that schools fire Black teachers. For those who were hired to teach in White schools, teachers reported hostility not only from White students but also from White teachers.

According to Madeline Will in *Education Week* (2022):

> Prior to Brown, Black teachers and principals comprised 35–50% of the educator workforce in 17 states with segregated school systems. Today, no state has anywhere close to those percentages, and nationally, just 7 percent of teachers and 11 percent of principals are Black.

Why is it important to tell this story? Too often, the lack of Black teachers and teachers of color is told as a personal deficit, a lack of motivation, or a devaluing of education in communities of color.

The practice of devaluing Black teachers post-Brown set the stage for generations of systemic racism in the form of teacher licensure. Matt Barnum (2017) wrote that teacher certification exams are keeping future teachers-of-color out of America's classrooms. There are a few obstacles that teacher candidates must face in the licensure process. In an analysis by the Education Testing Service, the researchers found that candidates of color were more likely to fail the basic skills test (Praxis I). Black test takers were 40% less likely to pass than White test takers, and Hispanic candidates were about 20% less likely. While there are multiple contributing factors to this data, including but not limited to lack of access in teacher preparation, most research has demonstrated that certification exams are not strong predictors of teaching effectiveness, yet these tests serve as gatekeepers to the teaching profession.

The COVID-19 pandemic had a major impact on the teaching profession. According to the Institute for Educational Sciences, 8% of teachers in public school exited the profession between 2020–2021 and 2021–2022. The Brookings Institute found that in January 2021, nearly one quarter of teachers indicated a desire to leave their jobs at the end of the school year, which was significantly higher than the average turnover rate of 16% before the pandemic. Initiatives that placed less emphasis on test scores and more emphasis on portfolio reviews, alternative assessments, and emergency licenses helped reduce some of the barriers to a more diverse workforce. Massachusetts, for example, in May 2025 approved an amendment for alternative assessments to the MTEL (Massachusetts Test for Educator License). The Center for Analysis of Longitudinal Data in Education (CALDER) found that teachers who entered the profession under alternative assessments and emergency licensure were, on average, more racially diverse than their peers who completed a traditional certification process. While there is ongoing research on the impact of assessment and licensure, it is important to remember that ongoing commitment to building the habits and skills of teaching, learning, and curriculum remain a steadfast focus to improving conditions in the field.

Teacher Preparation Programs and Identity Work

Normal Schools – programs that taught the norms of society – were originally established to provide systematic training of teachers. Their goal was to prepare teachers for work in the emerging Common Schools, or public schools, at a level beyond the simple grammar-school education many teachers previously brought to the classroom. Normal Schools prided themselves on their thorough, cohesive, and "scientific" curriculum. The first state-sponsored Normal School was established in Lexington, Massachusetts, in 1839. While the idea of Normal Schools achieved great popularity for a period and many states moved to set up their own schools, reformers around the turn of the twentieth century sought to professionalize teaching to a greater degree and established education courses at regular colleges and universities.

Today's teacher education programs are mostly found at colleges and universities, blending a liberal arts curriculum with rigorous teacher training.

This training often includes a minimum number of course credits along with supervised student-teacher training. While teacher training and preparation programs are widely found at colleges and universities, few incorporate an adequate amount of identity-based work. Many students report taking only one class related to "multiculturalism" and report that they were not required to teach in racially diverse school districts for their placement. How are current teacher education programs integrating and preparing teachers for a more diverse and identity-conscious approach? Shamaine Kyann Bertrand and Kisha Porcher (2020) identified that there are teacher educators who are serving as disruptors by redesigning courses in teacher preparation programs to better prepare White preservice teachers. They found that many teacher education programs, despite stated commitments to diversity, equity, and inclusion, reinforce the systems of White supremacy and White-centric teaching that go against their posted values. In addition, preservice teachers are not always given opportunities to learn about teaching in both urban communities and communities of color. Doing so, particularly when guided through the teacher preparation program, can help to name how identity is informing and impacting their teaching approaches, practices, and behaviors. Teacher preparation programs need to develop and implement courses that create and sustain equitable learning environments that are identity-conscious.

Teaching While White

One way in which identity shows up in teaching is related to race, specifically whiteness. If you have read the last few sections, and if you are White, you may be wondering, "So is this all a lost cause? Because of my racial identity, will I never be effective with students of color? Should I only be teaching White students?" That is a natural and common progression of questions. And let me be clear, "No." None of the research presented earlier says that you should not or could not teach students of color. It also does not mean that every teacher of color does this well either. And yet the research has demonstrated that there are differences. Therefore, it is important for all of us to understand how teaching and learning is informed and impacted by identity, specifically whiteness.

I am grateful for the work of Jenna Chandler-Ward and Elizabeth Denevi, who have spent decades exploring the role of White teachers in education. In the text *Teaching and Learning While White* (2023), the authors explore their own identities as White women and how the role of whiteness has impacted the classroom experience. They have taught in a myriad of schools – private, public, urban, suburban, primary education, secondary education, and graduate education – and they consistently see the need for White teachers to level up their understanding of race and their actions towards creating and sustaining a more racially conscious teaching and learning practice.

The authors highlight the importance of White educators developing explicit anti-racist teaching practices to create real equity in their classrooms and schools. Chandler-Ward and Denevi (2023) offer five key elements to address the social, political, and historical role of teaching:

1. I will teach the way I was taught unless I learn another way.
2. Teachers are not neutral; teaching strategies and methods are not objective.
3. We all speak from a particular standpoint based on our experiences.
4. There is no essential, observable single truth; rather, there are multiple truths.
5. Everything is not relative, but rather, we recognize that cognition – the way we think and learn – is dependent upon experience and context.

By engaging with these truths of our teaching practices, we can better see how identity shapes what we do and how identity can also be a leverage in changing, correcting, and remedying past harms that were done institutionally and systemically through schooling.

It might surprise you to know that I co-host the podcast *Teaching While White* with Jenna because, well, I am not White. However, as a person of color, I was socialized in a White system of education and have so much unraveling to do with my own beliefs about teaching, identity-consciousness, and practice. Because we "teach what/how we know," I learned about teaching and learning through the lens of whiteness. When I started teaching, I simply replicated what I knew, what I learned, and what I had access to. As I built more knowledge, engaged in more reflection, and identified key action steps to integrate a more identity-conscious approach, I began to unmask and reveal just how powerful the influence of whiteness was on my practices. In our podcast conversations, we talk openly about the challenges we face as teachers – both White and of color – and what it means to be more curious and critical in our work and of ourselves.

What might teachers of color want to consider in this landscape of whiteness? To start, if you were socialized through the United States education system, you likely also learned about whiteness in a very positive way. You likely were taught that White people founded the United States, that White people invented everything we use today, and that White people were the only ones who were smart enough to establish a government. If you grew up in a community and school like I did, you also read mostly White authors – and if you were lucky, an occasional writer of color was sprinkled in there. You were likely taught by White teachers who taught how they were taught. And you likely did not notice race or were conditioned to not notice it.

If you grew up in a school predominantly with students of color, but were educated by mostly White educators, you had the benefit of peers who were racially and ethnically diverse, but the power of the classroom was still in the hands of the teacher. And if you were educated by White teachers, the research has demonstrated that they are less likely than teachers of color to connect, support, and affirm your brilliance and joy.

Lastly, if you grew up with predominantly students of color and taught by teachers of color, you likely had the most exposure to literature, opportunities, and examples of excellence in our communities. You likely were supported, affirmed, and validated because of your cultural contributions – and not in spite of or as a token example of excellence. You likely had opportunities for criticality, rooted in cultural communities. You had opportunities to interrogate systems of oppression, of power, and of resilience.

And if you were White and grew up in predominantly White schools with predominantly White teachers, you had that too. Chandler-Ward and Denevi make the case for why interrogating race matters. It matters because identity matters in our teaching. It matters because the implications of identity are real. It matters because our approaches to teaching, whether we are conscious of them or not, are identity-informed. It matters because talking about whiteness and its impact matters.

Culturally Responsive Teaching

Given that there are differences in how people teach – informed and impacted by identity – it is important that we build skills in areas that have been proven to be effective in teaching. In this next section, we will explore the roles of culturally responsive teaching (CRT) and culturally relevant pedagogy (CRP) to frame our own approaches to reflection and practice. The ultimate goals of frameworks such as culturally responsive teaching and culturally relevant pedagogy are to create a learning environment that is identity-conscious, where students feel valued and can bring their whole selves into the learning community. An identity-conscious approach to culturally responsive teaching and culturally relevant pedagogy require us to reflect on our own connections to these frameworks.

My deep commitment to culturally responsive teaching is informed by the lack of opportunity I had as a young person to engage in content that included anything other than Eurocentric views. Though I was one of the only students of color in my classes in K-12, I never felt seen, heard, or valued in terms of my racial identity. Decades later, in my professional career, I was grateful to be exposed to Zaretta Hammond's (2014) framework for culturally responsive teaching. She focused her work on how the brain learns and how a responsive learning environment contributes to positive outcomes. Her framework is a helpful start for teachers ready to address and implement transformation in curriculum and ways of teaching, and I am grateful for the role she has played in my own understanding of teaching.

The Hammond framework addresses awareness, learning partnerships, information processing, and a community of learners and learning environment. As teachers bring *awareness* to their work, action items are focused on recognizing our own biases and our own cultural lenses. Teachers acknowledge the sociopolitical context around race, language, and culture and broaden their own interpretation of diverse students' learning behaviors. In *learning partnerships,* teachers reimagine their relationship with students as a partnership and balance giving students both care and push/challenge. Through these partnerships, teachers also take responsibility to reduce the social-emotional stress that can come with stereotype threats or microaggressions that can occur through readings, behaviors, and interactions with teachers and with others. Through *information processing,* teachers begin to take proactive steps to connect content with context, providing students the opportunity to tell stories from their own personal communities to process content. One key action in information processing is providing opportunities for students to process new content through methods that align with oral traditions of storytelling. Finally, teachers who are committed to engaging with culturally responsive pedagogy also commit to developing a *community of learners and learning environment.* Teachers create an environment that is both intellectually and socially safe for learning while also building space for sharing, voice, and agency. Knowing that classrooms are a space of learning, which can include mistakes, this aspect of the framework also includes restorative justice to manage conflicts and address/redirect negative behaviors. Embedded within these four quadrants are also practices of feedback, affirmation, conversation, and validation as ways to build relationships with students.

But Hammond makes clear what culturally responsive teaching is and is not. Educators who are introduced to the framework assume that culturally responsive teaching is simply about love and kindness – that we must create a community of belonging so that people can learn. True, belonging is a component of culturally responsive teaching; however, it is not the only part. Hammond states that culturally responsive teaching is as much about instruction as it is about relationships. Instruction matters – how the brain learns matters. How teachers engage in the information processing cycle, in the move from short-term to long-term memory, and in the practice of critical thinking are all part of the learning process. We must first recognize that the brain is designed to learn, understand how it learns, and then approach that learning from a culturally responsive and identity-conscious way.

Too often in my teaching practices I have seen the emphasis on relationships overtake the learning process. I have seen teachers who feel bad for students, who pity their circumstances, and who want to focus on the emotionality and relationships with students as a way to connect. However, when I have seen this go wrong, it has been because the teacher has stopped there – with the emotions and relationships. These teachers no longer hold high standards for students, no longer see their brains learning and processing, and fail to teach them the important skills needed for critical thinking. It is important, of course, that we understand the experiences of students. Yet emotions and relationships are not teaching, not critical thinking, and not learning. I have seen educators do more harm when they failed to help a student build critical skills for learning out of their own guilt for the difficult situations students experience. What does this look like? "He should just pass the class. He has a really difficult home life" or "She has experienced a lot of trauma this year. Let's go easy on her and not make her do the assignments." Life, circumstances, and conditions are an important part of human experiences. And as educators in the community, of course, we care about this. But, as Hammond warns us, only focusing on relationships at the expense of learning does not benefit the student. We must approach our teaching with a combined practice of care and skill.

Culturally Relevant Pedagogy

Developed by Dr. Gloria Ladson-Billings, culturally relevant pedagogy is defined as a teaching framework that empowers students intellectually, socially, and emotionally by using their cultural references to impart knowledge, skills, and attitudes (Ladson-Billings, 1998). This theoretical model calls for students to develop critical perspectives that challenge social inequality and inequity.

There are three main pillars in culturally relevant pedagogy (CRP): 1) fostering academic success, 2) developing cultural competence, and 3) fostering critical consciousness to challenge the status quo. In fostering student success, students are given opportunities to develop their ability to problem solve and provide reasoning. In developing cultural competence, students focus on both appreciating their own cultural backgrounds while also demonstrating a respect and curiosity for others. Finally, fostering a critical consciousness is about having opportunities to identify, analyze, and solve real-world challenges that result in social change. Gloria Ladson-Billings, who initiated the work on culturally relevant pedagogy, wrote "teaching that focuses on advancing student learning, developing cultural competence, and fostering critical consciousness is the only practice that accurately represents what is meant by Culturally Relevant Pedagogy" (Ladson-Billings, 2021, p. 351).

Like Hammond's critique of oversimplifying culturally responsive teaching, Ladson-Billings also warns against doing this work but failing to ground it in careful theory. The theory invites us to cultivate student voice and creativity. The theory invites us to open up possibilities for exploration and to do so by bringing one's whole self to the classroom environment. Taken together, culturally relevant pedagogy (Ladson-Billings, 1998) and culturally responsive teaching (Hammond, 2014) centralize teacher identity and students' academic outcomes. While models such as "multicultural education" or "diversity education" tend to focus on content, culturally relevant pedagogy and culturally responsive teaching focuses on the analysis of teacher identity, experience, technical skills, and readiness to affect change. Because of this focus on teacher beliefs, behaviors, and skills, these culturally responsive frameworks assert that teachers must be specifically trained to interrupt social and educational inequity (Gonzalez et al., 2005; Ladson-Billings, 1995; Villegas & Lucas, 2002).

Culturally responsive pedagogy places as much emphasis on teachers' stances – their thoughts, attitudes, behaviors, beliefs, and biases – as their techniques (Sleeter, 2012). Culturally responsive teachers are attuned to classroom practices that may contribute to inequity, and they are willing to build the habits and skills for reflection about their own identities. Teachers committed to culturally responsive approaches view their students as whole beings; they consider not only who the child is in the classroom but also the factors that impact that student's learning, engagement, and lives outside of school.

Proximity to Whiteness and White-Centric Cannon

In my small town where I spent my entire K-12 education, I learned very little about any communities that were not White. Part of this was due to the geographic location where I lived; I was in a town that was just 20 miles south of Boston that had a predominantly Irish and Italian community. There were very few people of color not only in the town broadly but also among the teaching faculty in the public schools. In my own K-12 education, I did not have a single teacher of color. The closest I ever came to this was when an Asian American guidance counselor joined the high school staff when I was a first-year student. But I never had him as a teacher nor interacted with him in any meaningful way.

I have noticed an interesting pattern when I have worked with students of color who attend not just predominantly but nearly all-White schools. There is this need to assimilate, fit in, and be proximate to whiteness. When I meet them during their school years, most of the students of color in these environments say that they fit in and do just fine in their social groups. They say they do not need other people of color nor need any special programs or opportunities. However, when I meet adults of color who attended these nearly all-White schools, many reflect on their experiences in secondary school as survival; they fit in because they had to. In hindsight, they wish they had the support they needed, especially when they did not even know they needed it. Many reported that they wish they knew how important it was for them to have mirrors – people who looked like them and understood their experiences.

I certainly fit this description. By the time I hit my preteen years, I was deeply ashamed of being Asian. No one else looked like me. No one else's family behaved like mine. No one else had food that smelled like ours. I begged my mom to pack me a roast beef deli sandwich with white bread every single day because that is what the other kids at the lunch table were eating. I wanted to wear the same brands of clothes my peers wore despite the fact that my parents had to clothe five children all in different stages of growth and development. I wanted to wear blue eyeshadow and dye my hair blond. I wanted to wear green mascara and light-pink lipstick. None of these, come to find out, were the right color palette for my dark, olive-brown skin and jet-black hair.

Though the physical effects were obvious, I also adopted thoughts, attitudes, behaviors, and beliefs of my White friends that, simply, did not serve me at all as a person of color. I used language that disparaged anything that was not mainstream White culture. I found myself echoing political statements and beliefs that were anti–people of color. And I distanced myself from anything that would make me stand out among my White peers. I started to take on anti-Black positions and beliefs, thinking that every Black person was somehow going to do something bad to me. When driving, I locked my car doors whenever I crossed from a safe suburb to the unsafe city (aka White suburb and Black city) that were separated by an imaginary and arbitrary line. It did not take long for me to be heavily influenced by misleading language of "reverse racism," particularly when it was time for my peers and me to apply for college admissions. Though there were very few students of color in my high school (and even fewer in any honors or Advanced Placement classes), somehow it was still "a Black person that took someone's spot" when college admission decision letters came out and a disappointed classmate opened their letter.

When you are a fish swimming in water, it is hard to know how to describe water. And yet, I always knew something was not quite right in these moments. I knew that I was not "one of them" (i.e., a White classmate), and yet I desperately wanted to not stick out. I craved my proximity to whiteness. I wanted to be in the inner circle. I knew that I already looked different from others at my school, and I needed to find ways to reduce this anxiety of being an outsider. So I began to adopt their behaviors. I began to believe their ideologies. I started to believe, as an Asian American, I was not only different but better than other people of color. I started to believe that I deserved things – that I was owed things – that others were not. I learned about the model minority myth without any critical context, nor did I have people who could help me see the truth of what it was – a calculated social tool used to divide Asian Americans from other communities of color by creating a false hierarchy for oppression.

An interesting thing happens when you start to believe you are an insider: everything validates you. When the books, histories, and contributions of White people were discussed in my classes, I wanted to feel like I was a part of that. I wanted to see myself as a part of those White successes, contributions, and scholarship. The fact that I did not learn anything about Black genius, Latinx achievements, Asian activists, and Native and Indigenous ways of knowing was the byproduct of it all. But, of course, I am not White. And the lack of knowledge, exposure, and understanding to anything other than White-centric education meant that I did not have access to developing necessary critical thinking skills required to participate in a democratic society – one where people can take multiple perspectives, interrogate those positions, and come up with their own opinions and positions on matters. I lacked this access for most of my formal education.

Now, as a teacher, I have the privilege and positional power to do something different. I get to position my Asian American identity as critical. The readings that I select for my classes are all rooted in critical thought and analysis, particularly from the lens of scholars and practitioners of color. Because many of my students were also socialized in a White-centric system, they have plenty of knowledge and experience with the scholarship of White authors, practitioners, teachers, and educators. However, much of their formal K-12 experience, like mine, lacked opportunities to learn from the perspectives of others. What I love about teaching in this way is that the students are constantly referring to their own educational experiences and applying this critical lens to what we are reading, particularly as it relates to the work they do each day with students.

As you might glean from this section, diversifying access to different experiences, perspectives, and methods is one way of not only disrupting a White-centric teaching, learning, and curricular experience but also allowing students to decide where they want to go from there. And I am proud to say that so many of the students do want to stretch the boundaries of identity-conscious teaching, learning, and curriculum. One key driver in that process is learning how to go from diversifying to decolonizing to indigenizing.

Decolonizing Teaching Practices

An emerging theme in teaching has been focused on addressing the White, Eurocentric models that serve as the foundation of education, particularly in the United States. The act of decolonizing education refers to the educational approach of dismantling narratives, perspectives, and knowledge structures that are only rooted in whiteness. Decolonizing education requires teachers to look outside traditional textbooks that have long left out the perspectives of marginalized communities, such as Native and Indigenous peoples, LGBTQ, Black, Latine, and Asian contributors to this country. In addition, a decolonial practice prompts educators to consider how their own learning and teaching practices were shaped by a singular story and perspective and how they may also be perpetuating the single story in their classrooms.

Decolonizing education is a response to colonial education – one in which colonizers came and took land, resources, and people from their environment and community. Many history books continue to rely on the founding of the United States, for example, with the journey of Christopher Columbus in 1492 or the Pilgrims at Plymouth Rock in Massachusetts. When we start with these stories as the founding of the country, we fail to acknowledge that there were communities present on this land prior to the arrival of Europeans. By including Native and Indigenous stories in our teaching, we remove the colonial narrative as the first narrative and situate it within a larger context of people, culture, and community.

Decolonizing education also requires teachers to challenge existing norms. Though decolonizing practices are identity-affirming, existing political and social pressures from some movements have deemed the teaching of pre-Columbus time as not important or, further, as "too woke." The challenges to culturally responsive teaching tend to be rooted in fear – fear that through education, others will understand that White people were not simply explorers but also colonizers to an existing society.

From Decolonizing to Indigenizing Teaching Practices

As we enter this next subsection, I first want to honor the labor of many Native and Indigenous scholars whom I have had the opportunity to learn with and from over the past 20 years. Many of these scholars exposed me to different frameworks rooted in both their lived experiences and their ancestral traditions. I am forever grateful for their encouragement to do a significant amount of work on my own – truly interrogating my own role in both decolonizing and indigenizing my teaching, learning, and curricular practices.

> Here are some of the scholars, practitioners, and educators that have influenced my own thinking, learning, and teaching related to Native and Indigenous communities. Please read their work, think critically about your own positionality, and create action steps for how you might want to engage further with the Native and Indigenous communities and the academy:
>
> - *Indigenous Motherhood in the Academy (2022).* Edited by Robin Zape-tah-hol-ah Minthorn, Christine A. Nelson, Heather J. Shotton.
> - Works by Dr. Stephanie Waterman, Ontario Institute for Studies in Education.
> - Works by Dr. Amanda Tachine, scholar, weaver, and storyteller, University of Oregon.
> - Dr. Claudia Fox Tree, retired Massachusetts educator, current facilitator and scholar, focus on K-12 education and decolonizing anti-racist education.
> - Institute for New England Native American Students, University of Massachusetts Boston.

What is the difference between decolonizing education and indigenizing education? Conceptually, decolonizing is disrupting, deconstructing, and detangling from colonial – White-centric – practices that have centered whiteness as authority, power, and superiority. Indigenizing represents a move to expand education's narrow conceptions of knowledge to actively include Indigenous perspectives, ways of knowing, and processes. In order to engage in indigenizing work, individuals and institutions must start a process of decolonizing their practices, policies, programs, and procedures and building knowledge of indigenous ways of knowing.

Much of these efforts are focused on curriculum. It is helpful here to describe and define what we tend to mean by curriculum. Curriculum tends to refer to the material that is taught in our schools. However, a more critical lens to this definition would include the phrase "curriculum tends to refer to the material that is selected to be taught." Who selects what students learn? How is that selection made? Often, educators believe that the way to decolonize curriculum is to simply replace readings, books, or concepts that centered White voices with those of people of color. However, this is not effective nor entirely true. Simply committing to representational diversity does not decolonize a curriculum. Teachers need to also engage with issues of power and purpose. For example, "Why were these the books that were chosen as standard reading in our schools? Why were stories of marginalized groups only told from a deficit lens?" Simply changing texts might increase diversity of authors; however, it does little towards decolonizing practices. Further, simply adding a few Native and Indigenous scholars in your readings does not indigenize a curriculum. To engage in indigenizing practices means to include voices, processes for reconciliation, and a shift to power to Native and Indigenous communities. Will this happen overnight? Of course not. But, together, we can begin to make progress towards providing students with a more critical, and historically accurate, lens of education and their societies.

In 2015, prompted by the Truth and Reconciliation Commission's Calls to Action, Canadian post-secondary institutions were asked to begin a process of ethically engaging Indigenous communities and Indigenous knowledge systems. A common practice that was developed was the speaking of land acknowledgements at events or gatherings. Typical land acknowledgements started with phrases such as "We are here on the unceded land of _____" or "Our university is on the original land of the _____." While this was a good start, land acknowledgements were soon used in performative ways – a way to signal that a university, school, or speaker was thinking about Native and Indigenous communities. However, Native and Indigenous scholars, particularly those from the Association for the Study of Higher Education (ASHE) Indigenous Scholars Collective, have invited people to shift from "land acknowledgements" to "land reflections" by providing additional questions for people to consider as they create their land acknowledgements:

- How your upbringing (home life, educational, ancestral) experiences inform your relationship to land.
- How your knowledge of the history of your campus and the roles you play on campus could inform your land acknowledgement.
- How the conference theme and conference location intersects with land acknowledgement practices.

Additionally, the ASHE Indigenous Scholar Collective recommends engaging in partnership with the local community. Specifically, they encourage building relationships with community members who have experience in land acknowledgement. The building process should be reciprocal and should include offering a stipend(s) and/or other forms of reciprocation to community members who participate in land acknowledgement practices.

As we work towards decolonizing and indigenizing our teaching, learning, and curriculum practices, it is important to consider how your own identities might inform and impact your approach to this work. Decolonizing and indigenizing your practices are not identity-neutral. Therefore, it is important you continue to build healthy habits and skills for an identity-conscious practice and your journey towards decolonizing and indigenizing your practices.

Teacher-Centered Practice

Visit any school website or mission statement, and you will likely encounter the words "student-centered" somewhere in the school's values. Student-centered is a healthy and important way to remember that our actions as educators and school leaders are, in the end, focused on outcomes and experiences for students. Yet teaching and learning is a bidirectional socialization process, one in which a reflexive community in a classroom informs and impacts itself. Student-centered tends to mean that we no longer pay attention to the identities and experiences of teachers because the only true focus should be students.

At nearly every school I have visited, leadership always uses the phrase "It's all about the students." Yes, however, what do we miss when we no longer consider the needs and identities of teachers? What can we gain from engaging in identity-conscious teaching practices that are focused on the identities of teachers?

In the piece "School Mental Health Is Not Just for Students: Why Teacher and School Staff Wellness Matters" by Nancy Lever et al. (2017), the authors explore how adults in school communities experience and process stress. While it is important that we focus on the experiences of students, too often we neglect the well-being of the adults in our building. And there are consequences for ignoring these needs. For example, in a study conducted by Gray and Taie (2015), 89% of teachers said they had "been enthusiastic about teaching when they started the profession but only 15% reported being enthusiastic at the time they completed the survey" (in Lever et al.,

2017, p. 6). Gray and Taie (2015) also found that the turnover rates are much higher in urban areas with up to 70% of the teachers leaving within their first year. This exhaustion that teachers feel is often expressed as "emotional numbing, feeling shut down, loss of enjoyment, lack of energy, increased illness or fatigue, increased absenteeism, and difficulty making decisions" (Lever et al., 2017, p. 7).

Multiple studies have demonstrated that teacher well-being also has an impact on the students. An interesting finding from a study conducted by Oberle and Schonert-Reichl (2016) found that teacher burnout appears to affect the stress levels of the students they teach, finding that teacher burnout explained more than half of the variability in students' levels of cortisol (a stress hormone) when evaluated in the morning.

Realizing that stress is a major part of the teaching experience and that the levels of stress and burnout are both unsustainable and negatively impactful, what are schools to do to ensure that teachers and adults can access wellness in their work? In 2005, the Directors of Health Promotion and Education (DHPE) created a comprehensive standard for school wellness that brings multiple resources for support. The DHPE recognized eight different components that should be a part of a wellness program to improve conditions for teachers, adults, and school leaders:

1. health education and health-promoting activities tailored to the needs of employees;
2. safe, supportive social and physical environments;
3. integration of program into the school/district structure;
4. linkage to other related programs (e.g., employee assistance programs);
5. worksite screening programs and follow-up care as needed;
6. individualized interventions to support employee behavior change;
7. education focused on helping employees make health care decisions; and
8. and evaluation and improvement process to help the programs improve their effectiveness (DHPE, 2005).

"It's all about the students" is certainly a phrase heard around schools. And yet existing evidence has demonstrated that schools and districts must also take care of the adults in the building. By doing so, we increase opportunities for the students, strengthen relationships, and increase learning outcomes.

Here are some examples of school initiatives that have prioritized the well-being of adults:

- Contract with an education assistance program (EAP) to provide outside support for employees to access a variety of counseling programs.
- Regular "health and wellness" fairs where employees can access all of the benefits that come with their insurance plans or membership in the school community.
- Workplace exercise programs that are offered either free of charge or limited fees.
- Honoring teacher's prep periods and not adding meetings or additional responsibilities to those times.
- Appreciation programs hosted by the parent council or advisory boards.
- Instituting wellness committees to get feedback from employees about what they want and what supports they most need.
- Inviting different experts in areas like financial planning, retirement, saving for college, etc., to support the lives of adults outside of school.
- Providing opportunities to build community together, such as "intramural" sports for adults, book clubs, and special interest activities and groups.
- Respecting sick time – keeping boundaries when employees are sick and allowing them to recover without the guilt of missing work time.
- Creating boundaries around "working 24/7" and instituting policies related to email responses after hours, etc.

Anti-Bias Teaching Frameworks

Over the past few years, teaching frameworks from an anti-bias lens have been central to professional development of teachers and school leaders. Many of these approaches mirror what you have been reading related to an identity-conscious practice – building awareness of our own identities and how they inform and impact how we act, interact, and see the world around us. Throughout this text, you have had opportunities to think deeply about your identities and how they show up in your teaching practices. But now that you have raised awareness of this work, what do you do with it?

Anti-bias teaching frameworks allow us to examine our practices with the goal of naming, owning, and interrupting bias in the classroom. Much of what we understand about anti-bias curriculum comes from Paulo Freire's notion of freedom, which means that individuals can deal critically and creatively with the world around them in order to transform their world (Freire, 2000). This freedom comes from rejecting the dominant narrative and replacing them with culturally reflective, culturally conscious learning. Rather than masking or hiding diversity of experiences, views, and perspectives, anti-bias curriculum amplifies these differences so that students can see themselves reflected in their learning. To responsibly provide curriculum that reflects this diversity, however, teachers have to examine their own biases, teaching, and decisions related to curriculum.

An important component to anti-bias teaching is the opportunity for teachers to reflect on their own practices, changes they make, and how their own socialization as teachers impacts their teaching. This process of reflection can be difficult, particularly for teachers who have not practiced the emotionality that might accompany this reflection. Often, teachers must confront their own schooling, the curriculum that was included or not included in both their schooling and in their teacher preparation programs, and address how their teaching practices may have perpetuated inequity.

Strategies for Implementing Anti-Bias Teaching

In addition to work that can be done in the early stages of teacher preparation programs, all teachers can benefit from ongoing commitments to reflection and engagement. There are a few strategies that teachers can implement to move closer to anti-bias teaching (Lin et al., 2008):

1. *Build the habits of engaging with parents and caregivers.* As early as teacher preparation programs, parents and caregivers should be invited to speak with teachers to present a parent perspective on education. Gaining a better understanding of what parents and caregivers are experiencing related to school, their support of their students, and their navigation of school challenges helps build sensitivity and understanding.
2. *Reflective journaling.* This strategy should not be reserved just for difficult times. Rather, the habit of journaling helps to externalize thoughts, challenges, and beliefs that teachers may have about their teaching. It also allows for a more subjective look at their experiences by giving the teacher the opportunity to read and reread their own thoughts.

3. *Role-play.* While role-playing can be difficult because of its hypothetical setting, teachers can benefit from trying on different ideas with trusted colleagues. Role-playing also allows teachers to say, "That didn't go as I thought. Let me try that differently." This provides healthy opportunities for trial and error in a controlled and safe environment for learning. These role-playing situations also allow for external feedback from other students, colleagues, and mentors.
4. *Peer learning communities.* Taking time to examine one's own practice can be helpful through structured peer learning communities. These can be initiated through book groups, article readings, or even taking current events in education and creating scenarios about how the events would play out in their own schools or grade-level teams. Building habits for peer learning communities create a culture of feedback, reflection, and exploration while validating the belief that we are all learning, growing, and developing as educators.

I facilitate faculty meetings not only at my own institution but at schools all across the country. I often ask, "What was one thing that you felt went well in your teaching practice this week? What was something you felt challenged by or felt could have gone differently?" Because everyone reflects on these questions and must respond (either in pair-shares or small groups), it requires teachers to come prepared to the meeting having thought about their teaching. After teachers share their examples from the week, they are then asked to reflect on their own roles, participation, and agency in those scenarios. "What role did I play in the successes this week? What role did I play in the challenges that occurred this week? How might my own identities and experiences inform and impact what occurred this week?" While we as teachers do not always have control over what happens outside of our classrooms, it is important to reflect on where our agency does fit, where we might be able to adjust or adapt aspects of our own teaching, and how the decisions we make in the classroom can shape experiences.

Reflection and Emotionality of Teaching

When you ask a teacher why they teach, a lighthearted (half-joking?) response is "Well, it's not for the money, that's for sure!" And the unfortunate truth in the United States (though not true in every country) is that the teaching profession is underpaid, undervalued, and underappreciated. According to the National Education Association, the average salary for a teacher starting in the United States in 2025 was $46,526, and nearly 70% of school districts in the United States still have starting teacher salaries below $50,000.

The District of Columbia has the highest average salary in 2025 starting at $63,373. Among the 50 states, California ($58,409) maintains the highest average starting teacher salary. The next two highest states are Washington ($57, 912) and New Jersey ($57,603). At the lowest end of starting salaries, Missouri ($38,871), Montana ($35,674), and Nebraska ($38,871), are the only states with the average salaries starting below $40,000 (NEA, 2026).

Why am I starting this section with a disclosure of pay? According to the Pew Research Center data (2024), only a third of teachers report they are extremely or very satisfied with their job overall. The report also finds that teachers are "satisfied with various aspects of their job, getting the most satisfaction out of relationships and the least satisfaction from how much they are paid." The highest level of dissatisfaction is over salary with 51% of teachers saying they are not too or not at all satisfied with how much they are paid.

Over the years, there has been increasing pressure on teachers to provide support beyond their training. For example, in recent years, teachers have had to serve as in-classroom counselors, crisis responders, and experts on disabilities. In addition, sociopolitical events, such as the "racial reckoning" of 2020, the global pandemic, and changing mental health needs, have required teachers to both engage with and manage trauma. As evidenced, many of these traumatic events have also included aspects of identity. In recent years, we have seen a rise in explicit racism and violence, anti-trans legislation, the militarization of the government against its people, and escalating financial instability.

One method of sustaining the work of teachers and educators is the process of connecting one's values to behaviors. Teachers should identify not only the habits and skills of engaging in culturally responsive teaching and culturally reflective pedagogy but also identify their personal values that help them sustain this work. Essentially, what drives a teacher to engage in the difficult work of CRT and CRP? How might educators navigate the complex feelings that can come with CRT and CRP? What support systems should educators have in place to navigate these feelings? The difficult work of sustaining these pedagogies requires a deep connection to the work.

Build Knowledge, Engage in Reflection, Move to Action in Teaching

In an identity-conscious practice, it is important to build knowledge, engage in reflection, and move to action. As we consider an identity-conscious approach to teaching, the framework applies directly. First, what do we need to know and understand about how identity informs and impacts teaching; the relationships among teachers, students, and families; and what it means to have an equitable classroom environment? It is important to address the historical context of teaching – who had access and who was denied opportunity.

Second, we need to understand our own positionality in this work. For example, how do our racial, ethnic, socioeconomic, religious, gender, etc., identities influence what we do, what we know, and how we teach? In this process, we can use skills such as proximity mapping (section 1) as well as helpful journal prompts. Yolanda Sealey-Ruiz (2026) refers to this as the "archeology of self" or a process of reflecting on our influencers in life. Reflection allows us to connect the historical context of teaching, the theoretical frameworks and ideologies around teaching, and connect these to who we are.

Third, we then move to action. What does this knowledge and our positionality call us to do? How do we, through an identity-conscious practice, create and sustain teaching environments that honor, value, and affirm identity? What needs to happen first? What skills and habits do we need to build and continue to keep the impact of identity central to our teaching? As we seek to improve our teaching practices and to work towards being identity-conscious educators, there must be evidence for improvement. We need to make plans for how to put this all into action.

However, as you are learning on this journey, even the acts of building knowledge, engaging in reflection, and moving to action are not identity-neutral. What individual people, identities, and experiences must do has to be rooted in our own consciousness of how identity shows up. As we continue this journey together, you will notice that this is not an instructive book on "how to teach, learn, and build curriculum." Instead, the work in this book asks us, "How do we engage meaningfully with teaching, learning, and curriculum through an identity-conscious lens?" Doing so requires us to reflect upon our own identities, ways we were socialized in education, and how our own experiences show up in what we do.

Activities for Identity-Conscious Teaching

In this section, you can be reflective of how identity may have shaped your own approach to teaching. Individually, complete these activities. If you can engage in dialogue or work with a peer learning community, there are discussion questions at the end of this section.

Activity 1: 5-Minute Writing Prompts

To build community in a peer learning group, these 5-minute writing prompts are helpful ways to engage in reflection about teaching. These prompts can be used 1) solely as a reflective exercise in a journal, 2) a think-write-pair-share, and/or 3) a large group share-out.

Prompt #1: Think about your "best moment" as a teacher or in a teaching situation. What happened in the moment? Use as many senses (e.g., feel, smell, sight, touch, hearing) to be as descriptive as possible.

Prompt #2: Think about a moment when you witnessed effective teaching. What was the scenario? Why did you identify that as an effective teaching moment? What did you feel when you saw or heard this?

Prompt #3: Reflect on a person you identify as a great teacher (does not have to be one you had nor someone real!). What do you feel when you think of this teacher? How does this person make you feel this way? What behaviors does this teacher engage in that you recognize as great teaching?

Prompt #4: If you were to explain the role of a teacher to these different ages, how would you describe the role of a teacher and why you want(ed) to be one?

1) To a 5-year-old
2) To a 16-year-old
3) To a peer
4) To someone significantly older than you

Activity 2: The Why

In the following space, allow yourself some time to focus on the *why* of your teaching by engaging in these prompt questions:

1. What was the moment when you decided to become a teacher/educator?
2. When you think about past teachers you have had, what qualities stand out to you (these can be both positive and negative)?
3. As you reflect on your current teaching practice, what are one or two things you know you are very good at doing?
4. As you reflect on your current teaching practice, what are one or two things you know you need to work on to be a more effective teacher?
5. As you observe other teachers, what do you notice in their approaches to teaching that you like or appreciate?
6. What has been the most helpful feedback you have been given about your teaching? Why was that the most helpful?
7. What was the least helpful feedback you have been given about your teaching? Why was that the least helpful?
8. If you could ask any teacher/educator/scholar for feedback on your teaching, who would you ask and why?

Activity 3: Pain and Gain

Teaching is an iterative learning process. It is not always true that "the longer we teach, the better we get" but rather "the longer we teach, the more quickly we can identify areas of improvement." But how do we get better at identity-conscious teaching? How do we more quickly identify areas of improvement in an identity-conscious practice? The following activity helps you to identify the "pain and gain" of an identity-conscious teaching practice.

Imagine that "staying the same" is your current teaching practice with no changes. In the "pain" column, identify what are the pain points for staying the same? What challenges will you face if you stay the same? What will be hard about staying the same? In the "gain" column, what will you gain from staying the same? How do you benefit from not changing your teaching practice to be more identity-conscious?

Now imagine you took the time to change your teaching practice to be more identity-conscious. What will be difficult or painful about making these changes? What challenges will you face if you do this? In the "gain" column, how do you benefit from developing a more identity-conscious teaching practice? What good comes of doing this?

Once you have completed your chart, take a moment to look at what you wrote. How might this chart inform your desire or commitment to engage in an identity-conscious teaching practice? What did you notice about these pain and gain points in your journey? Finally, what sense do you make of this chart? Is it directing you towards keeping your teaching practice the same or towards moving in an identity-conscious manner?

	Pain	Gain
STAYING THE SAME *(e.g., not changing teaching practices)*	*(I don't see much pain for staying the same other than teaching is getting a little bit stale; I'm starting to get a bit bored of the work even though I love the relationships with students.)*	*(If I don't change anything, I know this content so well that I don't need to prep anymore; I don't have to learn anything new; I can focus on things that are changing like student needs and SEL and other initiatives.)*
MAKING CHANGES *(e.g., teaching in a more identity-conscious way)*	*(This will take time and energy I don't have; this will require me to do a deep dive into my practice; doing this work would require me to do significant work during vacations or breaks when I really need to recharge and reset.)*	*(I've been falling into a routine, and this would help mix things up a bit and make work more interesting; I'd be exposed to new material; my relationships with students would improve.)*

As you create your pain/gain chart, notice we are not doing a pro/con list where the tendency is to simply "count" how many items you have in each box. Instead, we recognize that pain and gain are spectrums; so rather than simply counting the number of items in each box, we think about the impact of what we have written in each box.

Now that you have created your pain/gain chart:

- What do you notice?
- What stands out to you about these boxes?
- What feelings come to mind as you look at your chart?

Activity 4: Identifying Values

Values drive our behaviors. We work hard to keep what we value, and we also work hard to get what we value. This activity helps us identify what we value in our teaching practices and how we can sustain the work we do.

In my teaching, I value	What is the evidence of this?	When there is alignment, how do you feel?	When there is misalignment, how do you feel?	What behaviors can help you keep your values in alignment with your behaviors?
honesty	I do a check-in at the beginning of each class to get a sense of how the students are feeling and how prepared they are for class.	I really love when the students are honest that they are not 100% present coming into class. It helps me to modify my teaching practices, if needed.	I worry when students are not honest with me because I think that leads to them engaging in performative behavior. I want them to trust that I know how to support them even during hard times.	I have learned to model honesty with them. I let them know if I'm feeling a little distracted and what I'm doing to try to bring my focus back to the task at hand. I think they need to see that we are humans who are also working on better skills.

Activity 5: Rubric for Identity-Conscious Teaching

Use this tool to assess where your actions towards building a more identity-conscious teaching practice might be situated.

Identity-Conscious Teaching results in students feeling seen, heard, and valued through your choices and actions.	**Building Knowledge (I need to gather information about these areas.)** 1 | 2 | 3	**Engaging in Reflection (I am actively connecting how these areas are informed and impacted by my own identities.)** 4 | 5 | 6	**Implementing Action (I am using the knowledge and reflection to create actionable steps towards identity consciousness.)** 7 | 8 | 9
Content: the materials that I select reflect a range of identities			
Check for understanding: I use methods that affirm and validate the efforts made by students			
Scope and sequence: I effectively scaffold learning experiences related to identity through my teaching practices.			
Communication: I have strategies for addressing bias in how I call on students, engage in discussion, and communicate with them about important issues related to our class.			
Frameworks: I regularly implement anti-bias teaching frameworks into my lesson planning and classroom delivery.			
Emotionality: I regularly reflect on my teaching practices and highlight when I have felt strong emotions – positive and negative – in my teaching.			
Cultural Relevance: I teach multiple perspectives, ideas, and experiences to provide students the opportunity to think critically about how culture and identity are presented and discussed.			

Part II Discussion Questions

With a peer learning group, discuss the following questions:

1. What aspects of this section affirmed what you knew and experienced about teaching?
2. What aspects of this section challenged your thinking about teaching?
3. How did identity inform or impact how you experienced the activities in this section?
4. What parts of your identity felt close or proximate as you read about teaching? What parts of your identity did not feel represented or included in this inquiry about teaching?
5. What kind of support might you need on your journey towards identity-conscious teaching?

Part III

Identity-Conscious Learning

Key elements

- What theories can we use to inform and impact learning from an identity-conscious lens?
- What does culturally responsive learning look like?
- How does universal design support learning?
- How do stress, anxiety, and trauma impact learning?

Introduction

In March 2026, I had the opportunity to attend a conference called Rooted in Resistance, a celebration of Black and Brown educators who are deeply committed to justice. I attend a lot of conferences – sometimes every other weekend – and often serve as a keynote speaker or session facilitator. After 30 years in education, I am not usually surprised when I attend conferences, as the sessions are somewhat similar from place to place. However, at this conference, something very different happened to me.

I was sitting in the third row from the front during one of the keynotes. A brilliant scholar and activist, Dr. Curtis Acosta, a Chicano professor from Arizona, was on stage talking about resilience, learning, and education. Suddenly, projected onto the big screen, Dr. Acosta started talking about Filipino American activist Larry Itliong and the Filipino activist motto *isang bagsak*

DOI: 10.4324/9781003784739-4

("we rise and fall together"). Before I knew it, someone from another row was handing me a tissue. I had been crying. I did not even realize I had been crying because I was so locked in to Dr. Acosta's words and images on the screen. I had never seen a non-Filipino include Filipino activists, *isang bagsak*, or Filipino American movements on a stage. Not only did Dr. Acosta present the material but he also taught the entire audience *isang bagsak* so that they all understood what it meant.

Something happened to me in that room. I was both broken and healed at the same time. I think that is where my tears were coming from; my body was so confused as my mind was encountering something so personal. The physical response I was having was a release of decades of pain, isolation, and invisibility. This all happened in a matter of minutes, and it was because Dr. Acosta put a picture of my community on a slide, spoke words that were a part of my culture, and brought others into the experience. This is what a great teacher does. And this is what it feels like to belong.

From that moment on, I noticed my body relaxed. Yet I became very aware of how that relaxation allowed my brain to take in information, process it, analyze it, and apply it at such a fast rate. As you read earlier, this is not typically how my brain works. I have struggled with learning my entire life. I must work very hard to understand concepts and make sense of ideas that others seem to get so easily. I struggle with critical thinking and feel like it takes me longer than others to get from one point to another. But, in that moment, something changed. I got to experience a state of true relaxation in my mind. Because of that, I was thinking more clearly, hearing more carefully, and digesting more completely.

That experience at the conference made me reflect on all the times when learning just felt impossible for me. When I reflect on my educational experiences, K-12, undergraduate, graduate school, and even learning experiences I have now, I always wonder why I do not understand or comprehend concepts in the same way others do. Over the years, I have developed ways to compensate for my inability to think as critically as others or to process information as quickly. I am comforted by existing research demonstrating that there are multiple ways people learn, process information, and even demonstrate understanding. However, when I apply an identity-conscious lens even to those studies, there are still existing stereotypes about who learns well, why people learn, and how people learn.

Early in my teaching, I was not confident enough in my own application of the art and science of teaching. Instead, I relied on how I was taught, how I was presented information, and how I was told I should learn. Much of my early socialization related to learning was around content and memorization. As a teacher, I felt pressure to make sure that the students focused on content.

This meant creating a syllabus, nightly reading, and homework assignments that took hours to complete. I overloaded their brains with studies, research articles, and data charts. After a few times teaching this course, I realized that the students were not doing all the assigned readings. They were coming to class unprepared and skimming, if at all, the mountains of articles I assigned them. When I heard that the class was not doing a deep dive into all of the readings, I made judgments about them. I told myself a story that these students were not dedicated enough to their studies. I told myself that only serious students who read everything were going to advance in this field. I told myself that they were supposed to read everything, absorb everything, and process everything.

Ridiculous, right? And yet I often hear this from first-time teachers, particularly those who teach adults. There is this overwhelming need, for some teachers, to prove themselves in the classroom through a rigorous syllabus or pages and pages of content. But what is the real goal here? Is the goal to engage in meaningful student learning, or is the goal to prove you are a good teacher by making your class impossible? If I am being honest with you, I got very caught up in the idea that more difficult means better. I got very caught up in my ego being more important than what students were learning.

It took a few tries, but eventually, I got to a place where I put my own ego aside and started to focus on effective learning strategies for students. The strategies began with 1) overwhelmed minds do not learn well, 2) the readings should be manageable enough to do a deep dive of the articles, and 3) they should be learning skills, not just content. Clearly, the number of readings I was assigning and my expectations for how much time they should spend on my class was overwhelming, the amount of pages to cover was not manageable, and the skills they were learning were related to skimming and not critical thinking. I was not achieving the very learning goals I had set out for the students. Something had to change.

Before the next semester, I took time to build knowledge, engage in reflection, and create action related to my learning outcomes. I began to think critically about what the students needed to know in this educational leadership course. What was essential to their understanding of educational leadership? To do this, I had to engage in some deep reflection about how my own identities might be informing and impacting these goals. For me, I wanted them to read about leadership that was not just from a Eurocentric perspective; therefore, I prioritized articles that spoke to diverse leadership experiences and theoretical frameworks. I then assigned reflection papers that allowed them to critically connect what they were taught about leadership (typically Eurocentric models) and how these readings would be informing and impacting their existing knowledge. Then I had them create final papers about how they would enact their learning in their work – in other words, move to action.

Through this process, we can build critical skills related to educational leadership. The students discussed opportunities to connect theory to practice through not only their readings but also their practical work responsibilities. For those students who were experiential learners, they were able to connect real-world examples to the theories they were discussing about leadership. For students who learned best through verbal processing, I focused on opportunities to engage in discourseful discussions, position statements, and arguments about the readings and topics. And for those whose preferred learning styles were through reflection, I created opportunities for writing, thinking, and connecting. In essence, I was less focused on "Will they learn all the material?" to "Will they develop the skills to learn the material?" This was a pivotal moment in my approach to teaching and learning.

In this section, we will continue to explore existing literature on the ways of learning – not only how people learn but also the conditions through which people learn. While many resources address these theoretical and conceptual ways of learning, this section will also include how identity informs and impacts learning, leaning into how an identity-conscious practice shapes learning. The section concludes with a framework for assessing your own approaches to learning from an identity-conscious lens and an opportunity to identify action items to build better habits and skills for identity-conscious learning.

Theoretical Frameworks of Learning

About halfway through the semester with my students in the teaching, learning, and curriculum class, I often check in with them about how they are doing and the progress they are making in class. Many remark that the class is more than they thought it would be. They initially assumed it was a class just for those who wanted to be teachers, but they soon realized that knowing theories related to learning was helpful in their own growth and development. I heard students reflect on their own learning journey and what they might need to be successful in their graduate school journey. Many said they took for granted the science behind learning and that they felt a great deal of agency because of this new knowledge they were acquiring. Throughout the semester, I often heard, "Why didn't I know about these theories earlier? It would have been so helpful in my own learning journey." Well, we are here now.

While many of the students were well versed in different developmental theories, they had not spent a significant amount of time exploring the role of learning theories. And yet, once they made a connection to their own practice, the students began applying learning theory everywhere! Once they applied learning theory to their work, they noticed their workshops were clearer, the outcomes were more robust, and the students they worked with felt more empowered. Very quickly, the students in the class saw how important it was to not only build knowledge about different learning theories but also apply them in their practice of leadership. In this next section, we will cover some of the basic learning theories and, of course, apply an identity-conscious lens to how and why we learn the ways that we do.

Why Are Theories Important?

When I prepare workshops with school leaders, I often ask them what their priorities are for professional development and learning. They reply, "The faculty want tangible action items. They want to know exactly what to do when they get in the classroom tomorrow." I always appreciate this. I get it; we are busy. As teachers and school leaders, we do not always have the luxury and privilege to sit, think, reflect, and digest theories when we have real issues to manage in the classroom. Yes, and . . .

Theories help us understand how to look at things. Theories help us to understand why we do what we do and how we might approach change. They tend to form our thoughts and beliefs about learning and fill our toolbox with different strategies to use in our workshops, classrooms, and even department meetings. Despite the word "theories" attached to learning theories, frameworks on learning provide very practical approaches to teaching and learning. In each of these sections, we will learn practical strategies for how students best learn through these theoretical approaches. While there are many learning theories, in this next section, we will explore the most prominent learning theories: behaviorism, cognitivism, connectivism, constructivism, and humanism.

Behaviorism

Behaviorism is the idea that people learn by watching and observing. Founded by theorists such as John Watson, Ivan Pavlov, and B.F. Skinner, these theories emerged because of conditions in which young people demonstrated certain behaviors in reaction to their environment. In this approach, learning happens because a student is interacting with the environment and their responses or behaviors are being reinforced – positively or negatively – by their teacher. One of the more famous experiments related to behaviorism is that of Ivan Pavlov and Pavlov's dog. Pavlov taught dogs to respond to the sound of a bell by pairing the bell with food, leading the dog to salivate. Eventually, the ring of the bell would cause the dog to salivate in anticipation of food. Honestly, I understand this. When I was a student, and because I struggled with learning, I always felt sleepy and drained in class. The sound of the school bell always changed my response. I was suddenly more awake and energetic. I knew the bell meant we could go walk in the hallways or visit with friends by their lockers. Or, in the case of junior high school, if I timed it just right and left the room immediately when the bell rang, I got to catch a glimpse of Gregory, the boy I had a huge crush on, walk by me in the hallway. The very sound of the bell, every day, made my heartbeat just a little bit faster.

Behaviorism as a learning theory is most appropriately applied when considering actions such as positive reinforcement to validate and affirm student learning. Some of the most common examples include reward charts or verbal praise when a student gets an answer correct. Punishment is also a common tool used to shape behavior. For example, if a class does not behave, they might have recess taken away. If a child yells and screams to try and get what they want, a parent might remove something that child wants until they stop that behavior. While certain rewards and punishments may be effective in correcting behaviors, these methods are often critiqued for the lack of cognitive processing that is required in learning and behavior. And because rewards and punishments – along with a few other methods attached to behaviorism – tend to be temporary, the learning tends to be quite shallow because the student is only learning the behavior and not the purpose or reasons that drive the behavior.

In line with this critique, it is important to see why an identity-conscious lens would play a key role in understanding and utilizing behaviorism as a learning approach. While we all may have natural motivations – sleep, hunger, and shelter – not everyone is motivated by the same rewards and punishments. And not every behavior is desired in every culture, identity group, and background. For example, there are some teachers who reward or punish students based on class participation or the number of times a student speaks in class (e.g., answering a question, asking a question). Yet different cultural backgrounds, for example, encourage students to be more forthcoming and assertive in class while others prioritize respect and deference to authority in class. Still, others, regardless of cultural background, might need more time to process internally before answering or asking a question; yet the student who raises their hand first to speak is rewarded. These types of examples are helpful when understanding that behaviorism, as an approach, is also culturally situated. To engage from an identity-conscious approach would mean creating opportunities for people with different experiences, understandings, and backgrounds to still achieve. Specifically, in the case of class participation, a teacher should consider whether 1) only oral/verbal participation is what is assessed, 2) if there is enough wait time for those who benefit from more internal processing time to demonstrate their knowledge, and 3) if certain cultural backgrounds actually prioritize and privilege not being the first one heard. Yet to only assess on the fastest, verbal processing, and Eurocentric approaches to class participation creates inequity when rewarding through a behaviorist lens.

Cognitivism

Whereas behaviorism relies on the external reinforcement of a teacher (or outside influence), cognitivism places a stronger emphasis on the internal processes of the learner and how the brain organizes, stores, and retrieves information. The underlying principle of cognitivism is that learning is constructed and not merely absorbed. We tend to think of this approach as information processing.

Application of cognitivism would look like providing opportunities for problem-based learning. In the classroom, teachers using this approach should create conditions for active involvement of the learners. Teachers focus on the scaffolding of information by providing a hierarchy of knowledge acquisition. This means we are creating learning conditions that build skills for organizing information, processing, storing, and retrieving information. Teachers might ask questions like "What do we already know?" to activate existing knowledge from students. Then, through careful scaffolding, teachers would build upon that knowledge, create opportunities for processing the newly acquired knowledge, create reflective opportunities to connect existing knowledge to the newly acquired knowledge, and then provide scenarios for application. In cognitivism, students are focusing on tasks such as memory, thinking, and problem-solving and then applying this knowledge to new situations.

From an identity-conscious learning lens, it is important to acknowledge the role of the environment in this approach. In an identity-conscious practice, we are often asking questions about the influence of "thoughts, attitudes, behaviors, and beliefs," and cognitivism's approach to learning also considers these factors. Learners take external information and filter it through their own internal lens. Therefore, our existing identities and experiences inform and impact not only what we learn but also how we learn. Individual learners come to the environment with existing schemas, or categories, for how they view the world.

Constructivism

While cognitivism focuses on the inner mental processes, constructivism emphasizes how learners piece together their own understanding of reality through experiences and social interaction. In constructivism, students take an active role in their learning processes because they are building on existing context. While behaviorism is focused on the external evidence of learning, constructivism is focused on the internal processes of learning.

In practice, a constructivist approach to learning would include questions and interests of the students to build on their existing knowledge. Teachers create active classrooms of dialogue and discourse so that students can be exposed to new information, adapt or adopt their existing schemas to this new information, and then construct their own views or understandings about the information. A prime example of constructivist-based learning is problem-based learning, where students are presented with a problem, draw from both their personal and learned experiences, and construct solutions.

From an identity-conscious learning lens, the constructivist approach fits nicely with understanding how individuals make sense of the world. In this learning approach, it is understood that knowledge is personally, socially, and individually constructed. In a discussion-based lesson, students get to hear what other students think, how they approach the problem, and how their own backgrounds inform and impact their perspectives. This information sharing is important to developing critical thinking skills. Because identity informs and impacts these approaches to problems and solutions, it is important to amplify how individuals experience the world and contribute to diverse possibilities and how someone's own understanding of the world either aligns or contrasts with another's understanding.

Humanism

Humanism is considered a learner-centric approach to education and places a heavier emphasis on the learner rather than the methods of learning, content, or materials. This approach focuses on meeting the basic needs of students so that they can thrive in their learning environment.

Application of humanism-informed learning theories would look like students having more control over the pace of their learning. For example, it may mean that there are specific assignments in each week, but students can choose the order of those assignments and the timing of their actions in relation to a due date. Through this effort, the teacher should provide encouragement and support to motivate students and build their confidence not only with the material but also the skills they are developing. In this approach to learning, students are encouraged to ask questions, engage in self-directed learning, and contribute to new knowledge.

From an identity-conscious learning lens, humanism provides opportunities for the student to bring in their own experiences, cultural influences, and perspectives. Oftentimes, the types of questions that students ask are informed by what they have experienced, what they know, and what they are curious about. An identity-conscious practice encourages students to draw from these experiences and sees them as assets to their critical thinking and knowledge development.

Connectivism

Connectivism is a relatively recent theoretical framework in learning theory, as it takes in the role of technology into the learning practices. Connectivism places a strong emphasis on the ability to find and sift through information to conduct reliable research. While existing learning theories focused on the pre-digital age, connectivism focuses on the technologies of this tech-driven age.

Application of this learning theory requires the use and implementation of effective educational technology. Student learning goals should be related to finding information, critically assessing the sources of that information, and conducting accurate research. The focus of this theory is in real-world application through digital learning. And this digital learning happens through networks – both technological through applications and interpersonal connections. This can occur through gamification, simulations, and use of social media to expand beyond the immediate network.

From an identity-conscious learning lens, it is important to understand what students have access to related to their interpersonal connections. As we consider the role of social and cultural capital in the lives of our students, an identity-conscious lens encourages us to center what the students bring to the classroom and position these as assets in their learning. Though more schools are providing resources related to technology, it is important to remember that there are still great disparities related to access, equity, and opportunity related to technology. One of the lessons we learned from the COVID-19 pandemic and the impact on learning was that not every student had the same resources. During the pandemic, I partnered with schools who easily transitioned to online learning because all their students had the most advanced computers and internet access while other school districts were struggling to support students who were accessing Wi-Fi and internet from the parking lots of businesses and restaurants (if they were even open).

Adult Learning Theories

While the word "pedagogy" was coined to describe childhood learning, "andragogy" tends to be the word for adult learning. This may be a technicality, as many teachers, faculty, and professors at all stages of the P-20 educational spectrum still often use the word "pedagogy" to describe the teaching and learning experience.

Though the term andragogy emerged in the mid-1800s, it was not until the late 1960s that theoretical foundations of andragogy were applied readily to adult learning. The theory of adult learning is most attributed to Malcolm Knowles (1968), who laid out the conditions for adult learning:

- **Adults need learning that fits their busy lives.**
  A parent may have needs that conflict with their own school responsibilities, so it is important to be flexible while still having accountability measures.
- **They prefer learning that addresses real-world problems.**
  Provide opportunities to connect theory to practice by asking questions such as "How might this theory be applied to experiences you have in your work?"
- **They bring experience into every lesson.**
  Adult learners bring a wealth of experience to the classroom. Ask questions such as "How might this concept show up in your professional or personal life?"
- **They want to learn at their own pace.**
  Many adult learners also have responsibilities, such as families, caring for others, full-time jobs, etc. Provide opportunities to work at their own pace, to complete a significant amount of work when they have time, and also, to complete smaller tasks when there is less time.
- **Their motivation is mostly internal.**
  Not all teachers are motivated by "career promotion." Therefore, it is important to support motivation that drives them individually and internally. Provide opportunities for goal setting and time to create actionable steps to achieve their goals.
- **They need learning that meets them where they are.**
  In a school, you may have a diversity of experiences among the adults. For example, some are more technologically savvy, others may have more knowledge about certain literature or historical events, etc. It is important to create different pathways for learning that allow them to learn, grow, and develop.
- **Instructors need a plan that works for adults.**
  There are different ways that schools structure times for adult learning. Some only provide two to three professional development days a year. Others provide a half day of learning every two weeks. Those who are teaching adults must plan for effective learning given the time constraints, schedule, and processes for learning.

Because of the vast knowledge that adults bring to the classroom, instruction and learning should be focused on real-world learning, examples where students can draw from their life experiences. Teachers, for example, should be presented with a learning environment for professional development rooted in adult learning theories. Their time is limited, and the impact needs to be, well, impactful. Therefore, as designers of workshops or curriculum for adult learning, we must consider factors such as time restraints, relevance to their practice, use of technology (and perhaps hesitations about technology), learning styles and preferred modalities, and the conditions at which learning is optimized. For example, after 30 years of work in schools, I can honestly say that I am not really at my best at 3:30 P.M. after a long day teaching, advising, coaching, meeting, and writing up reports. After-school hours (e.g., 3:30–5:00 P.M.) tend to be the most common time for faculty meetings and professional development.

As we are building the skills for critical learning through an identity-conscious practice, it is important to situate the work of Knowles (1968) in a largely American, White context that is not necessarily applicable to global adult education. Critics such as Sandler Sandlin (2005) claimed that Knowles's model ignores the relationship of society and the individual's context of society. Knowles did not account for the different ways identities and experiences might approach andragogy and did not account for the ways in which race, class, and gender, for example, might shape people's approach to adult learning.

Culturally Responsive Learning

Over the past few years, there has been considerable attention to the role of culturally responsive teaching. One of my go-to texts is, of course, Zaretta Hammond's *Culturally Responsive Teaching and the Brain* (2014), which is a favorite among my students and me. There have since been many more texts related to joyful teaching, genius teaching, and culturally proactive teaching. What, however, is the role of learning, specifically the role of culturally responsive learning? What do these theories look like if we shift them from teacher to learner?

It should be stated that in a classroom, the teacher is responsible for creating the most inclusive and accessible environment for the student. Particularly for young children, it is a lot to expect that children can, or will, always advocate for themselves when it comes to cultural responsiveness of the teacher. In fact, most of my first two books address just how unwilling I was to speak up in class when I was younger. I was not only unwilling but I also came from a cultural community where challenging the teacher or even asking for anything other than what they had created was appropriate. However, as I move through my 30 years of teaching, I have seen some changes in the behaviors of students in the classroom. More students have realized their agency in education – that they are consumers as well as learners. When I was growing up, there were little to no resources about how to engage with teachers, to find my voice, or to even have confidence in the classroom. Today, students have access to videos, blogs, TikToks, reels, and essays from across the globe about how young people engage with their learning.

Partly informed by this change, young people are contributing to the classroom environment in more progressive and participatory ways. More students are growing up in project-based classrooms, Socratic seminars, and critical discussion groups. Their proximity to not only their classmates but to students all over the world has expanded their definition of "teacher as sage" and "student as passive vessel for knowledge." Because of this, it is timely to consider the notion of culturally responsive learning as it relates to the ways in which students arrive, develop, and grow in our classrooms.

If culturally responsive teaching is defined as integrating a student's knowledge, experiences, and perspectives into the lessons of learning, then culturally responsive learning is the bringing of that knowledge, experience, and perspective into the classroom. While most academic texts address the "teaching" part of culturally responsive teaching, few articles are found on the role of the learner in culturally responsive learning. Scholar and researcher, Mary Howard-Hamilton (2000) describes culturally responsive learning as a "liberatory practice" – one in which a student's psychological and cognitive complexities are valued in the classroom. Interactions with different ideas, opinions, and beliefs are a cornerstone of culturally responsive learning. While teachers might provide these opportunities through curriculum, discussions, and texts, students must also take responsibility for their learning through a willingness to engage in difficult conversations, to navigate the discomfort that comes with growth, and to think critically about concepts and ideas that might contradict what they have previously known or learned.

Much of culturally responsive learning is rooted in identity development theories such as the minority identity development theory (Atkinson et al., 1993) and White identity development theory (Helms & Cook, 1999). These theories help to guide the stages a learner may be in related to culture, identity, and race. Learners may interact with information differently based on where they might identify in these stage theories and what they may be ready to confront.

If you are interested in learning more about details of racial identity development theory and the impact on learning, here are a few that may be helpful on your journey. A useful activity is to take an identity development theory that is interesting to you, write a scenario that would demonstrate what this stage looks like in the classroom, and then provide a teaching tool or activity that would best shape an inclusive learning experience.

- Black racial identity development (Nigrescence model): William Cross (1971)
- White racial identity development model: Author: Janet Helms (1990)
- Asian American identity development model: Author: Jean Kim (1981)
- Latino/a identity development model: Authors: Bernardo Ferdman and Plácida Gallegos (2001)
- American Indian identity development: Author: Perry G. Horse (2005)
- Three-stage ethnic identity model: Author: Jean Phinney (1990)
- Biracial identity development model (BIM): W.S.C. Poston (1990)

Stage Theory of Identities and Learning

Identity formation is often categorized in relation to different stages of experience and understanding. Stage theories are often helpful when designing lessons related to identity because they help to locate where a learner (or group) may be at in their understanding of identity. Knowing how an individual (or group) may be approaching identity can help guide or shape the types of lessons or experiences you create for them.

Stage theories are also helpful when considering the types of cocurricular or social emotional learning that occurs outside of the classroom. These theories often approach identity development as a series of experiences that help move an individual from one perspective to another. While there are several different stage theories related to different racial and/or ethnic experiences, let us explore the format of Janet Helms's White racial identity development theory (1990) and connect it to learning opportunities.

Stage 1: Contact

In this stage, the learner has not had many experiences with – or contact with – issues of race and racism. The learner has minimal understanding of experiences of people of color and may even approach the world as "color-blind" (e.g., I don't see race. I just see people). They do not consciously notice race and are uncritical of how identity informs and impacts the world around them. In a class setting, the learner may display ignorance from a lack of exposure or criticality about the world around them.

Stage 2: Disintegration

In this phase, the learner has had some exposure to issues of race and starts to experience discourse. They see racial differences and are growing conscious of how these differences are shaping people's experiences, but they still are not sure how to reconcile these differences. They still may choose their own racial group (whiteness, in this case) over people of color but start to experience some conflict around their thoughts and feelings. In a class setting, a learner may be able to articulate inequity but still not choose to be placed in a position where they will not benefit. They may intellectually demonstrate an understanding but are unable to reconcile personal feelings about a situation.

Stage 3: Reintegration

In this stage, the learner has been exposed to different sources of information related to race, has been exposed to inequities and differences, and may have even struggled with morality and decision making. However, because this information can be emotionally, psychologically, and morally challenging their previously held beliefs, some learners may regress back to a White-dominant approach, blaming minoritized communities for their own demise rather than seeing a failure of systemic inequities.

Stage 4: Pseudo-independence

The learner may have had an experience that impacted them deeply in their feelings towards race and racism. Perhaps the learner has had a personal interaction that caused them to explore their own thoughts and beliefs more deeply. But this stage is marked by the learner's ability to see similarities between themselves and other communities (or individuals). They are still not ready to understand the political, social, and structural aspects of race and racism, but they are moved by personal and individual narratives and experiences where they can connect to others. In the classroom, this might look like deeper interpersonal relationships with other classmates or efforts to develop relationships with those who are different from the learner. However, the understanding of race only goes as far as the individual relationships that the learner is willing to cultivate.

Stage 5: Immersion/Emersion

As the learner experiences, learns, and reflects more, the learner begins a personal exploration of their own thoughts, attitudes, behaviors, and beliefs. They begin to question what they learned about race and how their biases are formed and perpetuated. Learners begin to take a more active role in their understanding of race and racism and think critically about the compounding social and political structures that have shaped institutional racism. In class, this may look like deep critical thinking, analysis, and synthesis about issues related to race and racism.

Stage 6: Autonomy

In White racial identity development, this stage marks the experience of the learner understanding their identity as a White person. They move through feelings of guilt, conflict, and denial of the reality of race and embrace that race and racism are social constructs with real implications. This stage marks the acquisition of knowledge about race, ethnicity, and culture while also the desire to learn and reflect more. The learner begins to take on a non-racist White identity and seeks opportunities to be exposed to more readings, discussions, reflections, and actions related to dismantling racism.

Though each stage theory differs in the learner identities (e.g., racial identities), the theories tend to take on similar markers of differences from stage to stage. In each of these phases, teachers can create lessons, readings, discussion questions, and activities that align with where students may be at in relation to the different stages. Learning about identity should be an experience that brings people together – an opportunity to discover that differences are good, beneficial, and contribute to critical thinking skills. As we use identity stage theory in our learning goals, we center the identities of the students, find ways to shape learning that starts where they are, and create opportunities for growth.

Learning and Universal Design

While stage theories help us to tailor different experiences and lessons based on individual needs, universal design is meant to create opportunities for all. At its core, universal design is understood to be "conditions that are usable by all people without or with limited accommodation." Something that is universally designed should work for as many people as possible regardless of any type of disability. For example, a universal design works for anyone who may:

- Have blindness or loss of sight
- Low vision or limited sight
- A hearing impairment
- Deafness or loss of hearing
- A need for physical assistance from a caregiver or aide
- Difficulty moving the neck, head, or parts of the body
- Difficulty sitting or difficulty standing
- Sensitivities to chemicals
- Differences in body size, shape, height, or weight
- Limited coordination
- Limited mobility
- And others

How is universal design different from our current requirements related to the American with Disabilities Act (ADA)? The ADA allows for separate accommodations – for example, separate parking spaces that are designated with a blue placard or sign and bathroom stalls that have larger spaces, stability bars, and automatic flushing. Universal design indicates that all conditions – parking, bathrooms – can be used by all people no matter where they go.

In 1997, the Center for Universal Design at North Carolina State University developed a list of key principles in universal design:

1. Equitable use – does not segregate others but allows for safety and privacy
2. Flexibility in use – the design allows for adaptability of space
3. Simple and intuitive – the design should be easily understood and used regardless of an individual's experience, knowledge, or language
4. Perceptible information – the design allows for multiple modes of learning and allows for greatest legibility
5. Tolerance for error – the design minimizes hazards, and any hazards are eliminated, isolated, or greatly reduced
6. Low physical effort – the design can be used efficiently with minimum of fatigue
7. Size and space for approach and use – the space is appropriate for posture, mobility, sight or senses, and options for different abilities

While many of us work in buildings and classrooms that are only recently designed or even retrofitted to meet ADA compliance, there are examples of institutions, schools, and organizations that have not only committed resources but also aligned their mission, vision, and values with universal design. For example, some schools who utilized "left hand" and "right hand" desks replaced them with flexible and moveable desks that can be used by either type of writer but that also allow for easy movement behind the desk.

Universal design in learning not only includes the physical environment but also proactively plans for different ways of learning, processing, and comprehending information. Three key components to universal design in learning align well with the identity-conscious practice of building knowledge, engaging in reflection, and moving to action. In UDL, it is important to create opportunities for the students to engage with the material, reflect on the material, and put that learning into action.

At its core, universal design considers the different types of learners in your classroom as well as your own needs and approach to teaching and learning. Universal design in learning means that we are not making identity and experience an afterthought; rather, identities and experience are at the forefront of planning.

Effects of Stress and Anxiety on Learning

Throughout this book, we have made the argument that anxious or overwhelmed minds do not learn as well as ones that are in a positive and supportive environment. Anxiety can impact the learning process in significant ways. First, anxiety impacts focus, and focus is necessary for executive functioning. We have often heard of the "fight, flight, or freeze" response that has served evolutionary purposes for survival. These instincts, when a student is feeling threatened or anxious, can also show up in the classroom. When the body and mind are more concerned with survival, there is little room for creativity, executive functioning, and focus.

So what can teachers and leaders do to reduce stress and anxiety in the classroom? We need to make sure the learning environment holds an appropriate amount of stress and challenge to grow but not so much that it pushes a learner into a state of survival. And, unfortunately, telling a student (or anyone, for that matter) to "just relax" is not often a helpful solution. Students experience stress and anxiety when they believe that the learning environment is not conducive to mistakes and errors. I shared a story earlier in the book about how I never raised my hand in class because I was always worried that my answers in class were going to be wrong. I shut down, turned inward, and just tried to get through the day. It would have certainly helped if anyone else in the class made mistakes or if the teacher encouraged us to get answers wrong.

The students I teach come into the classroom with a lot of anxiety. Some express that they are anxious because they have not been a student in a classroom in a very long time. Others worry that they will have to be perfect in their answers because they are required to be perfect at work. Some say that they learned that the classroom is where the "teacher is always right," and by raising their hand to ask a question or get clarification, they feel it might insult the teacher.

One of the phrases my students know me to repeat is "How would you know if you've never done this before?" For example, "How would you know how to write a 20-page paper if you have never done this before?" or "How would you know what a problem statement is if you have never constructed one before?" Phrases like these give them permission to come into the discussion not fully understanding how to do something. These phrases give them permission to experiment, to get answers wrong, and to try on something new.

Another way that I try to reduce anxiety and stress in my classroom is to create moments of predictability. Because I work with adult students who have to leave their workplaces, possibly arrange for childcare, and then commute to class in the late afternoon, I am well aware that life interferes and that, sometimes, they are a few minutes late. The students who needed to arrive late always apologized profusely and said they felt bad or guilty about missing the first few minutes of class. They always worried about what they had missed. In response to this, the first ten minutes of my class are very predictable. I have writing prompts and/or reflection questions at the start of each class. Though they change from class to class, students know that the first few minutes of class will always be about reflection, a peek at the agenda for the day, and an opportunity to warm up and talk with each other. I am not encouraging students to show up ten minutes late to class; instead, I am creating structural opportunities for those who are on time to engage in previewing the class while those who are occasionally running late know exactly what they have missed. This predictability helps to reduce stress and anxiety at the beginning of class.

Stress and anxiety can cause a few behavioral challenges. For example, emotional dysregulation is when stress has the power to disrupt emotional response and regulation. Students might display behaviors of anger, sadness, and anxiety that get in the way of focus and engagement. Cognitive impairment is also a result of highly stressful and anxious environments. For example, students may have trouble with memory, recall, and focus.

Trauma-Informed Learning

It seems over the past decade that the term "trauma-informed" has become mainstream in our lexicon. I hear it at all the schools I visit. And it has become a badge of honor for teachers when they say they are "trauma-informed teachers." But what is trauma-informed learning? And how might identity inform and impact this approach?

Trauma-informed teaching, by definition, is the recognition of how aspects of trauma (e.g., abuse, violence, chronic stress) affect behavior, development, and performance. It is one way of shifting individual attention (e.g., "What is wrong with you?") on a student to take in the totality of experience, background, and experience (e.g., "What happened to you?"). The focus for teachers is on creating a safe and caring environment by building relationships, creating conditions of trust, and supporting student's self-efficacy. Decades of research has demonstrated that students who have adverse childhood experiences (ACE) are more likely to exhibit negative behaviors at school. Adverse childhood experiences can include but are not limited to physical, emotional, or sexual abuse; physical or emotional neglect; and dysfunction in the household due to mental illness, divorce, addiction, incarceration, or violence in the home. Given the rise in children who have experienced ACEs, it is likely that teachers are also seeing the impact of ACEs in their classroom.

One way that teachers most commonly interact with the impact of trauma is through learning. A 2023 report by The Children's Bureau outlined how brain development is impacted as a result of trauma, stating:

> the specific effects of maltreatment may depend on factors such as the age of the child at the time of maltreatment; whether the maltreatment was one-time or chronic; the identity of the person involved in the neglect; whether the child had a nurturing caregiver or supportive adult; the types of interventions used; and individual and environmental factors.
>
> (p. 5)

Maltreatment can impact brain structure and activity, as well as behavioral, social, and emotional functioning.

In the classroom, major symptoms of trauma may look like cognitive delays, difficulty forming or maintaining relationships, inability to predict or make inferences, and wariness of the future (Maryland State Education Association, 2017). Students who experience trauma primarily need to feel safe. When they feel threatened or frightened, they may experience the fight, flight, or freeze response. Students may display these responses even when other children who have not experienced trauma do not, therefore making their behavior seem out of the ordinary. In addition, students who demonstrate trauma responses in the classroom may shut down or even attempt to overcontrol situations. They might turn to physical and behavioral responses, such as aggression or hyperactivity. Students often feel their emotions are overwhelming, and therefore, it is important that adults identify these emotions.

> As an educator or someone who works with students or perhaps vulnerable adults, you are likely a mandated reporter. A mandated reporter is a person required by law to report reasonable suspicions of child abuse, neglect, or harm to appropriate authorities. While this section is focused on the impact of trauma on the classroom, mandatory reporting does vary by state. Please report any suspicions of harm, abuse, danger, or neglect to the appropriate authorities.

While each student's situation is different and may require different strategies to meet their needs, there are a few overall recommendations for how to support trauma-informed learning in your classroom. *First, focus on relationships.* Make sure each student has a strong relationship with a trusted adult in the school, building, or program. *Second, be supportive.* Young people need to know there is someone they can count on who understands who they are. *Third, make emotions a regular occurrence.* If students build the habits of naming their feelings and emotions in your classroom, they are more likely to express them and be better at talking about them. *Fourth, practice mind-body activities.* This helps students build awareness of the connection between their emotions and their physicality. *Fifth, create clear community expectations in your classroom.* These should include absence of bullying, teasing, threatening, or engaging in ways that put others down. Students should take ownership of their community and how others feel in the classroom.

With the rise in adverse childhood experiences (ACEs) and the impact on the classroom, teachers are being asked to do more with their students.

Because of this, many teachers take on the secondary trauma – the exhaustion, fatigue, and emotional drain of caring for others. Knowing that you shape the community in the classroom, students need you to be aware, calm, and knowledgeable about trauma. This takes a great deal of energy and effort, and therefore, teachers need to create real structures for their own care too. It is important to find ways to engage with your own emotions, behaviors, thoughts, and feelings particularly as you care for others.

Without a doubt, identity informs and impacts our experiences with trauma, our reactions to trauma, and even those who get help for trauma. According to the Center for Disease Control (Terlizzi & Norris, 2021), a little over 25% of women receive mental health treatment compared with 14% of men. White adults (20%) were more likely and Asian adults (4.8%) were least likely to have received counseling or therapy. According to the 2021 National Survey on Drug Use and Health, 21% of Black and African Americans had a mental health concern, yet only 39% of them received mental health services. The suicide rates for Black Americans rose 58% between 2011 and 2020 with death by suicide being the third leading cause of death for Black Americans ages 15 to 24. According to the 2024 Trevor Project Survey on the Mental Health of LGBTQ+ Young People, there is a significant association between anti-LGBTQ+ victimization and "the disproportionately high rates of suicide risk – that far too many young people struggle to access the mental health care they need." As we consider the role of schools, the same survey found that "more than half (54%) of transgender and nonbinary young people found their school to be gender-affirming, and those who have affirming environments did report lower rates of attempting suicide." This finding is significant as we continue to address the impact that schools and school climate have on the safety of young people.

While these statistics continue to demonstrate the pervasiveness of the impact of racism, sexism, homophobia, and transphobia, the implementation of trauma-informed teaching and learning has helped to address some of these issues in the classroom. For example, the Trevor Project survey found that of those LGBTQ+ young people enrolled in school, 32% were verbally harassed because people thought they were LGBTQ+ and 21% reported not being allowed to dress the way that fit their gender identity and expression. In addition, 9% of respondents stated they believed they were disciplined more harshly because teachers/staff thought they were LGBTQ+. For the respondents who were enrolled in schools, "Transgender and nonbinary young people who had access to gender affirming clothing gender-neutral bathrooms at school, and had their pronouns respected by the people they live with had lower rates of attempting suicide compared to those who did not." Finally, the report stated that "Most LGBTQ+ young people who attended school (78%) reported having at least one adult at school who is supportive and affirming of their LGBTQ+ identity."

As we consider the multiple identities and experiences in our schools and classrooms, it is important for teachers and educators to create and sustain identity-conscious environments for all young people to not only survive but also to thrive. We can create positive classroom communities by developing intentional and meaningful relationships with students in a way that signals they belong in the classroom, school, and community. We can make choices about our teaching practices to validate and affirm the differences in our classrooms. And we can create opportunities for learning through different theories that build on the strengths of each student. At the same time, we must also take care of ourselves as teachers, leaders, and humans. The work of teachers has changed and shifted over the years, and there has been an increased need for us to pay attention to the social, emotional, psychological, and physical safety of students. This work can be taxing, particularly as we face the fatigue of not only content teaching but also the additional social and emotional work. Individual practices such as reflection, connection, community-based learning, and restoration can help us sustain ourselves in the process. In addition, institutions must also create opportunities, spaces, and intentional times for teachers to rebuild their energy stores for this difficult work. It is possible for us to shape healing-informed communities for all.

Activities for Identity-Conscious Learning

Activity 1: 5-Minute Writing Prompts

To build community in a peer learning group, these 5-minute writing prompts are helpful ways to engage in reflection about learning. These prompts can be used 1) solely as a reflective exercise in a journal, 2) a think-write-pair-share, and/or 3) a large group share-out.

Prompt #1: Think about your "best moment" as a student and learner. What made this your best moment? What did you feel? What did you experience? Be as descriptive as possible.

Prompt #2: What was something difficult you learned? What did you feel as you were learning it? Did you ever want to quit learning that skill? What happened as you progressed through your learning?

Prompt #3: Removing the limiting thought "I am too old to learn this," what is something you would like to learn to do? Why do you want to learn this? What would change, if anything, if you learned this?

Prompt #4: As you think about someone in your life, what do you wish they would or could learn? Why did you choose that? What would occur if that person learned that skill?

Activity 2: Trauma-Informed Learning

The purpose of shaping a trauma-informed learning environment is to foster safety and security so that optimal learning can occur. Read the following scenarios and identify possible factors that can be changed or adjusted to create a safer, trauma-informed, learning environment that focuses on healing and engagement.

A. Students in Professor Jones's class use the syllabus to keep track of the daily readings and assignments. Coming to class prepared means reading the assigned articles or sections that are due, creating critical questions, and preparing talking points. However, Professor Jones leans into a very conversational style of class and "goes with the flow" of the class. Sometimes, this means the material that was assigned was not covered in class that day. The class readings are a few weeks behind, but students worry about not doing the readings for the assigned day out of fear that Professor Jones might say, "Let's just jump to the readings listed for today," even though they might not have covered previous readings.
B. Ms. Holmes assigns a lot of group projects which are done in class. She believes that collaborative learning is the best way to engage with each other and relies on the groups to challenge each other. This level of engagement requires the students to really know the content so that they can engage with each other critically. Some students have complained that, when they are in their groups, some of their classmates do not carry their weight. This requires the others in the group to do extra work. The lack of participation by some of their classmates also means that the group is not always productive during their discussion times. While some students have complained about the dynamic in the class, Ms. Holmes has remained steadfast in her approach, learning from published research about the importance of building collaborative skills through group processes.
C. The school policy is that students must always be in a classroom during classroom time. Keeping the students in the classroom has been one strategy for reducing loitering in the hallways. In recent years, this loitering has often led to fights, damage to school property, and disruptive behaviors outside of classrooms. One student,

Erin, has repeatedly asked the teacher to use the bathroom. Erin asked a few minutes into class but was told that they should have gone during the passing period. Erin grows increasingly agitated, and the teacher begins to wonder if Erin even needs to go to the bathroom or if there is something more mischievous at play. Erin is unfocused, physically agitated, and sighing loudly. Erin asked again towards the end of class but was told that they needed to wait until class was over. Erin has now reached their limit and begins yelling at the teacher, standing in the middle of class, and yelling profanities.

D. Professor Morales starts each day predictably with a writing prompt on the board. The prompt is typically connected to the lesson they are focusing on that day. The students know to come into the classroom, take out their notebooks, think about the prompt on the board, and then spend the next five minutes writing a response. When students enter, Professor Morales usually plays upbeat music to raise the energy in the room and to get the students' attention. Most of the students seem to appreciate the energy and often come into the room dancing and moving. Some other students sigh when they come into the room and take a significant amount of time to get started on the brief writing assignment. While some classmates are busy writing and even moving their bodies while answering the prompt, other students are barely writing a few words on their papers before the five-minute time is up.

E. It is midway through the semester, and Henry is missing a significant number of written assignments. The teacher is aware that Henry is going through a lot at home with many transitions impacting day-to-day stability. She gave Henry quite a bit of leeway to finish assignments knowing how challenging his home life is. Yet it is the midway grading period, and the teacher needs to submit a grade for the progress report. At this point, Henry's grade is an F. But the teacher knows how demotivating it will be for Henry to see that grade, and she is trying to keep him engaged in class. While Henry does participate in class verbally, gets along with other classmates, and often volunteers to be helpful, he is still not turning in his written work. With grades due, it is difficult to assess his learning since no written assignments have been turned in.

Activity 3: Stage Theory, Learning, and Classroom Activities

Research one of the many identity development theories that can inform and impact the learning experience. There are a few examples of racial identity development in the following example. You may research other identity development theories related to gender, sex, etc.

At each stage of the theory, identify the characteristics a learner might present at that stage. Next, identify a teaching opportunity that supports that student and also challenges their thinking and learning.

Example:

White identity development theory (Helms, 1990)

Stage	**Description**	**Learner Characteristics**	**Teaching Opportunities**
Contact	Contentment with racial status quo	"I don't need to learn about African American writers."	List the author and books students have encountered. Ask, "What do you notice here?"
Disintegration	Confusion and distress	"This is an American literature class. I'm upset that you're making me read Black authors."	"Let's look at some terms. What does 'American' mean? Where does that come from? Who defines it?"
Reintegration	Glorified ideals of one's social group	"It's not my fault that Black authors didn't get book deals or get published back then."	"What were some of the barriers that Black authors faced? What were the barriers that White authors faced? How might those exist today?"
Pseudo-independence	Making exceptions that are more inclusive but still fit a singular narrative	"I'm okay with reading a few books by Black authors because these ones are famous and everyone knows them."	"Let's look at popular lists like the *NY Times* Best Sellers or Goodreads Top 20 or Book Recommendation Lists. What do we notice? What do we see? Who do we see often? What might contribute to the repetition?"
Immersion	The search for a more compassionate approach	"I guess it's good to read other ideas and experiences."	"What are the results of us only reading one type of author or one experience? What could happen if we read other authors and other experiences? What might occur? What might we feel?"

Stage	Description	Learner Characteristics	Teaching Opportunities
Emersion	The appreciation of the difficulty of doing the work	"This is hard, but I do like having conversations with my classmates about their thoughts and opinions."	"What agreements might we need or understandings we have about difficult conversations? What do you need in order to feel you can share your opinions and thoughts?"
Autonomy	A commitment to avoid contributing to oppressive conditions	"I am rethinking how I learned and what I learned. I am going to dive deeper into literature and authors who are not White to better understand both myself and the world around me."	"Where might we find lists unlike the ones we saw earlier in this process (e.g. *NY Times* Best Seller)? How difficult/easy was it to find those lists? What do you notice about those lists and the ones we found earlier? What might be challenging in sustaining the practice of reading different authors than those who are likely privileged?"

Activity 4: Rubric for Identity-Conscious Learning

Using the text from the section on identity-conscious learning, reflect on where you may be at this stage of learning: building knowledge, engaging in reflection, or implementing action. Provide examples in the space later of what you need to work on, focus on, or improve.

Identity-Conscious Learning **Students are presented with multiple ways to learn, think, process, and share that are culturally aligned.**	**Building Knowledge (I need to gather information about these areas.)** 1	2	3	**Engaging in Reflection (I am actively connecting how these areas are informed and impacted by my own identities.)** 4	5	6	**Implementing Action (I am using the knowledge and reflection to create actionable steps towards identity consciousness.)** 7	8	9
Theories of Learning: I connect my practice with existing scholarship related to learning theories.			

Identity-Conscious Learning **Students are presented with multiple ways to learn, think, process, and share that are culturally aligned.**	**Building Knowledge** **(I need to gather information about these areas.)** 1 | 2 | 3	**Engaging in Reflection** **(I am actively connecting how these areas are informed and impacted by my own identities.)** 4 | 5 | 6	**Implementing Action** **(I am using the knowledge and reflection to create actionable steps towards identity consciousness.)** 7 | 8 | 9
Universal Design: I start my teaching, learning, and curriculum to be accessible to all learners, limiting the need for accommodations because my practice is universally designed.			
Identity Stages: I use identity development theories in my work to inform effective scope, sequence, and scaffolding for lessons.			
Stress and Anxiety: I engage in practices that help to minimize stress and anxiety so that students can learn in a relaxed and confident manner.			
Trauma-Informed Learning: I actively create learning opportunities that are informed by theories and practices related to trauma and trauma reduction.			

Part III Discussion Questions

With a peer learning group, discuss the following questions:

1. In your own educational experiences, how was learning approached or modeled for you?
2. As you consider the students in your class(es), what barriers do you identify to engaged learning?
3. How might identity be informing and impacting the learning experience in your class(es)?
4. Knowing that cultural connection can foster learning, what barriers and opportunities do you identify in your class(es) that might be impacting learning?
5. What support do you need to take your next steps in identity-conscious learning?

Part IV

Identity-Conscious Curriculum

Key elements

- What theories guide the development of identity-conscious curriculum?
- What do we need to do to decolonize and indigenize curriculum?
- What is the role of ethnic studies as an identity-conscious curriculum?
- What are the impacts of curricular joy and curricular violence in our schools?

Introduction

As a doctoral student, I was interested in the experiences of educators who identified as Asian Americans and Pacific Islanders. Knowing that we are underrepresented in the field of teaching, learning, and curriculum *and* that we tend to need role models, I wondered, "Why and how did Asian Americans and Pacific Islanders choose to be educators despite a lack of representation?" I spent six months interviewing Asian American and Pacific Islanders in graduate programs in education and leadership, hoping to find a common inspiration and thread. Through an approach called life history methodology, I asked them questions about their earliest educational experiences all the way to the current day. One particular prompt I ask is "Share with me what you learned about Asian Americans and Pacific Islanders when you

DOI: 10.4324/9781003784739-5

were growing up." I assumed that their answers about the curriculum would vary based on their geographic region; areas with more Asian American and Pacific Islander representation would, of course, cover more material related to these communities. I was surprised to find out I was wrong. No matter where the participants grew up in the United States, we all learned the same four things about Asian Americans and Pacific Islanders:

1) We were told that we were associated with war and violence – Korean War, Vietnam War, and Pearl Harbor attacks.
2) We were told Chinese people built the railroads, but many details were left out of these lessons.
3) We were enemies of the state and needed to be imprisoned and heavily guarded.
4) We were the model minority.

I grew up in Boston, where there is a robust Irish and Italian immigrant history. By comparison, Asians were a historically recent immigrant group to the Boston area, and I just assumed that I never learned about Asians or Asian Americans because of where I lived. In my research, I was excited to interview participants who lived in California, specifically the Bay Area, where there is a dense population of people from Asian and Pacific Islander heritage. I wanted to know if they had more opportunities to engage with a culturally reflective curriculum, one that included the stories of Asians and Pacific Islanders. So, it was surprising to me when participants from those regions – regions that had proximity to vibrant Asian and Pacific Islander contributions – also named those same four major themes about our people.

How, and why, was this the case? How did students in such racially diverse communities still only learn about the same limited messages that I received in my largely homogenous, White community? How did their proximity to places like Angel Island or Japanese internment or generations of Asian immigrants not impact what they were learning in the classroom? How were they learning the exact same things I was learning in my predominantly Irish and Italian town? It was this inquiry that really fueld my desire to know more about the impact of curriculum and identity-consciousness.

Curriculum serves as an important pathway for education, critical thinking, and opportunity. It is through our curriculum that we build learning outcomes, create engaging activities, and ask probing and curious questions. Curriculum is the way we explore the world through the stories of others. What is the impact of a curriculum that only validates and affirms one narrative, one story, and one perspective? How do we, as educators and school leaders, shape identity-conscious curriculum, evaluate curriculum for its cultural relevancy, and adjust when needed? In this section, we will have the opportunity to explore some theories related to curriculum and learn how to assess curriculum for identity-consciousness.

Theories Guiding Curriculum

The field of curriculum studies emerged in the nineteenth century after the wave of open, free public schools emerged. Primarily, students were focused on rote memorization and mental discipline. Beginning in the twentieth century, the shift from repetition to engagement began to take shape in schools. Researchers such as Francis Parker and John Dewey emphasized child-centered learning and the role of behavior and social interactions. In the twenty-first century, much of curriculum studies was focused on individual differences, diverse learning styles, and the integration of technology in learning experiences. In 1918, Franklin Bobbitt wrote *The Curriculum: A Summary of the Development Concerning the Theory of Curriculum*, which emphasized that students would be trained in tasks that would prepare them for careers. This served as the basis for many vocational educational programs that emerged. It was not until 1949 when Ralph Tyler wrote *Basic Principles of Curriculum and Instruction* that we see the beginning of what we know today as lesson planning, including learning outcomes, goals, objectives, activities, and assessment.

Missing from many of the early theoretical approaches to curriculum, of course, was identity. In the 1970s, with the emergence of the Civil Rights Movement, student protests, and women's rights, there was a great deal of pushback on the largely White, Eurocentric, male-focused curriculum that was standardized in many schools. The existing curriculum lacked an interrogation of power that guided the decisions made in schools. Student protests, cultural, and political movements pushed institutions to look deeper into how decisions are made and how lives are impacted through the process of schooling. This application of critical theory pointed at how curriculum was influenced by classroom dynamics, power, and hierarchy.

Curriculum Theories and Development

In the previous section, we were introduced to a few learning theories that shaped the current landscape for our understanding of education. However, what is the connection between learning theory and curriculum development? How do these two concepts inform and impact each other? One of the challenges is that learning and teaching have been historically disconnected.

One reason could be that the fields of learning and teaching are often housed in different fields; for learning, most of the work has been in the field of psychology, and teaching has been mostly housed in education. In addition, when teaching is only treated as an art, we then neglect learning and cognition as a science.

Informed by researchers such as Dorothy Huenecke (1982) and Joseph Schwab (1973), Glatthorn et al. (2005) posits there are four main categories of curriculum theories that are informed by their domains of inquiry:

Structure-oriented theories are concerned primarily with analyzing the components of curriculum and their relationships with the educational environment. A primary question in this theory is "How do teachers make decisions about the curriculum?"

Value-oriented theories are concerned primarily with analyzing the values and assumptions of curriculum developers. These tend to be critical in nature and attempt to sensitize educators to the power differentials in society. A primary question in this theory is "How do schools consciously or unconsciously influence students to fit into social roles that are informed and impacted by race and class?"

Content-oriented theories are concerned primarily with the major sources that should influence curriculum content. They are focused on the inclusion of child-centered theories and knowledge-centered theories. A primary question in this theory is "How does the content in this curriculum align with the structures of the discipline?"

Process-oriented theories are concerned primarily with the descriptive nature of curriculum, focusing on how curricula are developed or how they should be developed. A primary question in this theory is "How are decisions about curriculum being made and demonstrated?"

While these theories guide how curriculum might be developed or approached, the role of identity continues to be important in these processes. For example, we should ask key questions about who gets to make decisions and how those decisions are turned into curriculum. It is important to ask which identities tend to influence these decisions and how identity informs and impacts content. It is important to examine how power and privilege create spaces at decision making tables for some and not all.

One remedy to this challenge is to center curriculum development, design, and theory that includes scholars of color who not only approach this work from an identity-conscious lens but who also provide actionable ways to disrupt a Eurocentric approach to curriculum and include more voices, experiences, and approaches to teaching, learning, and curriculum.

While early curriculum theories by White scholars have been elevated, it is crucial to include the approaches to curriculum that have been presented by scholars of color. Here are a few scholars to read and complicate the existing approaches to curriculum and curriculum studies:

W.E.B. DuBois and Carter G. Woodson – critiqued White-centric education
Kimberle Crenshaw – influenced critical pedagogy through critical race theory
Mary McLeod Bethune – civil rights leader who developed curriculum for Black students
Gloria Ladson-Billings – leveraged student cultural backgrounds through culturally relevant pedagogy
Amanda Tachine – Navajo scholar focusing on Native education and experiences in higher education
Theodorea Regina Berry – scholar focused on the significance of Latine presence/absence in the curriculum
Sohyun An and Noreen Naseem Rodriguez – authors of an Asian American studies K-12 framework

Identity-Based vs Identity-Conscious Curriculum

In my work with teachers and schools, I am often asked, "Liza, are you suggesting I redo my entire curriculum to be focused on identity? I didn't complete teacher training in identity work; I completed my teacher training in (fill in the blank with subject)." I understand this is often an assumed takeaway from workshops on identity. Teachers, who are already overwhelmed with external metrics, classroom management, social emotional approaches to behavior, parent and caretaker inquiries, and teaching evaluations, often hear "identity-conscious curriculum" and assume it means a complete overhaul of what they are doing.

To demystify this approach, let us first think critically about the differences between identity-based curriculum and an identity-conscious curriculum. An identity-*based* curriculum is one in which identity is the central content through which all teaching and learning is expected to occur. Identity-based curriculum has lesson plans, outcomes, sections, exercises, and reflection questions rooted in particular identity categories (e.g., race, class, gender, religion, ability, family structure) and the goal is to build knowledge, engage in reflection, and move to action work that advances the visibility and position of different identity categories. The focus is on the categories themselves.

It is true that there are curricula that are identity-based. Oftentimes, curriculum related to advisory, health and wellness, identity or affinity groups, and even classes focused on social emotional learning (SEL) can very much be identity-based. An identity-*conscious* approach to curriculum, on the other hand, is not focused on identity being the outcome. Rather, an identity-*conscious* curriculum focuses on identity being a part of the process. An identity-conscious approach to curriculum is the vehicle through which your existing curriculum is taught. For example, a mathematics teacher needs to create and sustain opportunities for students to learn addition, subtraction, geometry, calculus, sine, and cosine. An identity-conscious approach to curriculum asks whether there are opportunities for learning about identity through the work of math. An easy example might be teaching the same addition/subtraction lesson but adding culturally reflective or culturally curious examples. Instead of asking what 4 bananas + 5 bananas is, substitute "bananas" for "plantains," a food more commonly used in the Caribbean or parts of Africa. A more advanced example might be using percentages to measure the change in water depth as time passed during the tragedy of Hurricane Katrina, calculating the speed and pressure at which the existing dams likely gave way, and analyzing the demographics of the areas most impacted. An identity-conscious approach disrupts single-story content and, for example, includes the roots of science and math in Mayan and Arab cultures rather than limiting historical context to Greek and Roman contributions.

In conversation with students about their learning experiences, many of them commented that "they always learn about communities of color as a separate section. For example, if they are in United States literature (U.S. Lit) class, there is a special section about Black authors. Yet when they are discussing White authors, the teacher does not refer to that section as the 'White author section.'" An identity-conscious approach would 1) acknowledge the dominant positioning of whiteness as "United States literature"; 2) include authors of color as integral and embedded in U.S. Lit while also discussing the challenges and barriers they overcame to be recognized; and 3) engage the students in critical thinking related to race, publication, authorship, and privilege.

The Role of Culturally Relevant Curriculum

It is well understood that a culturally relevant curriculum provides students the opportunity to both be reflected in their learning and to learn new things.

Culturally relevant curriculum, which is also known by other terms such as *culturally responsive teaching*, *culturally sustaining pedagogy*, and *culturally relevant pedagogy*, relies on the work of Rudine Sims Bishop (1990) and the concepts of "windows, mirrors, and sliding glass doors" (p. 3) and Geneva Gay (2002), who defines culturally responsive teaching as "using the cultural characteristics, experiences, and perspectives of ethnically diverse students as conduits for teaching them more effectively" (p. 106).

While a culturally relevant curriculum may seem applicable to literature and humanities classes, it is also meaningful in STEM subjects (Brown et al., 2019). Brown et al. (2019) found that "STEM education research has found that cultural relevance has the potential to allow students to gain a rich understanding of STEM and its connection to their local communities" (p. 776). Brown et al.'s (2019) study identified "how teachers' desire to improve in their science and mathematics teaching practices could lead to changes in pedagogical practices" and that:

> nearly all the participating teachers, regardless of their time teaching, never received training about how to apply Culturally Relevant Education (CRE) principles. For them, CRE instruction was an ideology that lived in the realm of English education and did not have pragmatic STEM applications.
>
> (p. 799)

Further, research by Allen et al. (2022) confirms that "irrespective of the level of intervention, teachers remain a central point of focus when considering best practices for fostering school belonging," and therefore, the focus on raising the skill and capacity for teachers in racial equity frameworks and curriculum is a major lever in shaping belonging.

The Fight for Ethnic Studies and Its Outcomes

One way in which the voices of people of color have been included in education is through the interdisciplinary field of ethnic studies. The field of ethnic studies contributes to transforming academic culture through the courses and pedagogy that speaks to the needs, demands, and marginalization of communities of color by recovering and reconstructing the histories of those Americans whom history has neglected; identifying and crediting their contributions to the making of U.S. society and culture; chronicling protest and resistance; and establishing alternative values and visions, institutions, and cultures (Hu-DeHart, 1992). Asian American studies, specifically, includes the social, cultural, economic, political, religious, and environmental consequences in the demographic shifts in the U.S. due to immigration and refugee resettlement; addresses the exclusion of Asian Americans in the binary dialogues on race and diversity that tend to focus on the Black-White racial paradigms; focuses on the results of globalization of capital and labor; and includes social and psychological impacts of traumatic experiences of refugee communities (Chang & Kiang, 2002, p. 151). In a qualitative study by Kiang (1999), alumni at one campus who had taken at least Asian American studies course indicated that the course had "much" or "very much" increased their understanding of the immigrant experience (91%), raised their awareness of racial stereotypes (86%), enabled them to make friends with people different from their own backgrounds (70%), and helped them interact more confidently with other Asian Americans (83%) (Chang & Kiang, 2002, p. 152).

Samuel Museus, Professor of Ethnic Studies at the University of California San Diego, wrote in 2008:

> The desirable course of action [to impact dominant cultural attitudes and beliefs] is to cultivate institutional cultures in which the salience of racial stereotypes and prejudice are minimized and students of color . . . believe themselves to be unique individuals and valued members of the broader campus community.
>
> (p. 8)

Ethnic studies seeks to recover and reconstruct the histories of those Americans whom history has neglected; to identify and credit their contributions to the making of U.S. society and culture; to chronicle protest and resistance; and to establish alternative values and visions, institutions, and cultures (Hu-DeHart, 1992). By increasing opportunity to, knowledge of, and experience with different racial and ethnic groups, schools can positively impact the attitudes of students, who have not been given opportunities to study, learn, and discuss their histories (Talusan, 2016).

The implementation of identity-conscious curriculum, teaching, and pedagogy are aspects of culturally responsive teaching. According to researcher Geneva Gay (2010):

> culturally responsive teaching is validating and affirming because it acknowledges the legitimacy of cultural heritages of different ethnic groups; builds bridges of meaningfulness between home and schools experiences as well as between academic abstractions and lived sociocultural realities; uses a wide variety of instructional strategies; teaches students to know and praise their own and one another's cultural heritages; and incorporates multicultural information,

> resources and materials in all the subjects and skills routinely taught in schools.
>
> (p. 32)

Ethnic studies seeks to recover and reconstruct the histories of those Americans whom history has neglected; to identify and credit their contributions to the making of U.S. society and culture; to chronicle protest and resistance; and to establish alternative values and visions, institutions, and cultures (Hu-DeHart, 1992). By increasing opportunity to, knowledge of, and experience with different racial and ethnic groups, programs can positively impact the attitudes of students, who have not been given opportunities to study, learn, and discuss their histories.

The fight for ethnic studies in education continues to be one of the most important battles in teaching, learning, and curriculum. One of the most recent – though long fought – battles for ethnic studies was won in Tucson, Arizona, and brought forth by Dr. Curtis Acosta (whom I wrote about earlier), activists, students, and faculty. Dr. Acosta was teaching Mexican American studies and reported that the benefits of ethnic studies on student experiences and outcomes were positive, disrupting negative academic trends for Chicano students, such as dropout rate, homework completion, and college enrollment rates. Despite the positive impacts, the ongoing racism that was pervasive in the school district led to the banning of all Mexican American studies classes in the district. Acosta and the team of activists filed legal challenges, and after many years, the ban was overturned in July 2013. According to Acosta, the fight for ethnic studies was not just about the content but it was also about "rehumanizing education that . . . created freedom" (Fong, 2014).

Decolonizing Curriculum

As teachers seek to diversify the curriculum, it is important to focus not only on the content but also on the process. One helpful understanding of pedagogy comes from Tintiangco-Cubales et al. (2010), who write:

> Pedagogy is a philosophy of education informed by positionalities, ideologies, and standpoints (of both teacher and learner). It considers the critical relationships between the PURPOSE of education, the CONTEXT of education, the CONTENT of what is being taught, and the METHODS of how it is taught. It also includes (the IDENTITY of) who is being taught, who is teaching, their relationship to each other, and their relationship to structure and power.
>
> (p. viii)

Therefore, while providing culturally relevant content has been proven to create greater connections for students of color, this content is limited by the preparation and will of those who teach it. To truly decolonize the curriculum, we must also turn our attention to teacher preparation. Studies by Baptiste (2010) and Daus-Magbual (2010) showed that teachers must also engage in deep reflection about their own identities in connection to culturally relevant content, addressing their comfort level, the relationship of this content to their own narratives and lived experiences, and building relationships with students in the class. In studies (e.g., Pollard & Ajirotutu, 2001; Sanders, 2009) where teachers were not provided opportunities to reflect, connect their identities to content, and address their own pedagogy, student behavior in these classrooms was observed to be disruptive; activities were teacher-centered; and there was little interaction between teachers and students. This reinforces the need to not only address curricular issues but also teacher identities, preparation, reflection, and connection to be effective.

Decolonizing curriculum and teaching are focused on eliminating racism. It is designed to develop critical thinking and understanding and help students understand how to transform the world around them (Tintiangco-Cubales et al., 2014). Decolonizing curriculum and pedagogy "allow for a systemic critique of the traumatic history of colonialism on native and Third World peoples and, subsequently, healing from colonial trauma, including the trauma of having learned to see oneself as academically incapable" (Tintiangco-Cubales et al., 2014, p. 8).

One way in which the ideology of whiteness is embedded in our schools is the practice of not talking about race or avoiding conversations about race. Some schools have leaned into the belief that "talking about race is racist." However, engaging in issues of race in school provides young people (and adults) the opportunities to build the habits and skills for talking about race. Talking about race brings about greater racial understanding and helps to address institutional practices that might be contributing to inequality and inequity in our schools. Another way in which the ideology of whiteness shows up is in the treatment that White people do not have a racial identity. In fact, research by White scholars and practitioners (e.g., Ali Michael, Robin DiAngelo, Tim Wise) affirm that being White had a lot to do with their understanding of the world. Schools can help students see themselves in a larger racial context and begin to understand how race and racial identity has also shaped their lives. Beverly Daniel Tatum (2007) suggests that White students can identify as White and work against racism. Schools can be ideal places for young people to develop meaningful cross-racial friendships and relationships, learn historical truths about the impact of race in our country, and work towards a more racially just system. This work stands in stark contrast to the colorblind ideology that was a dominant viewpoint for decades, where race was not discussed or acknowledged as an influential factor in decision making (Michael & Bartoli, 2014). Today, schools are leaning into identity-conscious practices to build skills and habits of racial awareness.

Curricular Violence

When I attend parent-teacher conferences at my children's school, I often have to sit in the car for a few minutes and engage in deep breathing. I know what I am walking into when I go into these situations. I know that the teachers are going to share their standardized curriculum, learning outcomes, and highlights of the program. And, far too often, I realize they are teaching the exact same content in the exact same way that I learned back in the late 1980s. They are still learning about U.S. history that starts with colonization and enslavement. They still are engaging in a section of text that covers the entire Civil Rights Movement in a few days. They are still learning that Japanese internment was the only way to keep Americans safe. They are still learning by the "sage on the stage" method and not building skills for criticality.

One night, after yet another frustrating back-to-school event, I had posted on social media looking for advice from teachers about how I can respectfully push back on their existing curriculum, like AP U.S. History. Some responded with "Liza, I teach AP U.S. History, and I really wish there was anything to be done. Unfortunately, we are assigned a particular textbook, and we are told we have to cover certain things that are on the assessments." Others replied, "Yes, I get it. This is why I try to bring in supplemental texts or go out of my way to provide a different perspective. But no matter what I do, it is still an add-on and not central to the existing textbook that we are required to use." As someone who has taught in independent schools where teachers are often given a great deal of flexibility and autonomy, I realize that the structural inequality of public and private education are great influencers in this conversation too.

This is what we mean by curricular violence: the negligent manipulation of academic experiences that cause psychological, emotional, or intellectual harm to students. Much of what we see in the curriculum suppresses cultural differences other than whiteness and Eurocentric perspectives, leaving diverse communities to compare their own experiences with this single narrative. Recently, I asked a high school graduate to reflect upon their high school experiences. I asked the question, "When I say the term curricular violence, what does that mean to you?" The student was able to answer it in a way that aligned with the current definition. After learning that they believed their high school curriculum had multiple examples of curricular violence, I asked, "What would be different if it did not include curricular violence?" The student paused for a few minutes. Finally, the student replied, "Yeah, sorry. I'm struggling with this question because I can't imagine it any differently. Like, I can't even begin to imagine that they would teach AP U.S. History (APUSH) differently. I can't even imagine a learning environment in which I didn't always wonder, 'I bet there is another side to this story.'"

As we were having a conversation, another student came over and asked what we were talking about. "AP U.S. History class," said the student I was interviewing. "Oh my gosh," replied the student who arrived. "I swear, I learned so many problematic things in that class. Like, my teacher was always running out of time in class and ended up using very short-cut terms and phrases. For example, one time, my teacher referred to the fact that the French colonizers who arrived in America were friends with the Indigenous people. I was like, I don't think that sounds right. And my teacher replied, 'I mean, right. I guess they were less mean than other colonizers, but we don't really have time for that.'" The two students shook their heads, laughed uncomfortably, and then said, "I guess that's curricular violence, huh?"

As I talked to more students about their experiences with curricular violence, many made a point to say that they "felt bad" for their teachers. They knew their teachers were competent, knowledgeable, and excited when students showed curiosity or made connections. However, for the students I spoke with who had standardized assessments as the final project, many just felt their teachers were under such pressure to meet the metrics of the tests rather than meet the needs of the students.

While curricular violence can be the misrepresentation of culture, facts, histories, and relationships, it can also include the complete omission of information. I remember the moment when I was in my doctoral program that I read about the Indian boarding schools. I had graduated from high school, undergraduate, a master's program, and was two semesters into my doctoral program when I was even exposed to this information. To add insult to injury, I grew up in Massachusetts – a state that takes its name from the tribal community originally of the land, has a Native symbol on the state seal, and is the home to one of the most famous (and mistold) stories of Plymouth Rock and the first Thanksgiving. And yet, I did not even have information about these atrocities until I placed myself in the 1% of the worldwide population in this doctoral journey. This erasure and intentional omission sparked my commitment to elevate and amplify Native and Indigenous voices, histories, and perspectives in my own curriculum and content at much earlier stages. The complete erasure, and the ongoing violence, that is perpetuated against Native and Indigenous students in our schools – and of non-Native students – limits what we can learn, understand, think critically about, and act.

In 2010, authors Erhabor Ighodaro and Greg Wiggan published the book *Curriculum Violence: America's New Civil Rights Issue*. In this book, the authors unmask and reveal the experiences of African American students in schools who have long been educated with a curriculum that has centered White, middle-class cultural values and outcomes. Scholars often refer to this as emotional destruction that compromises the well-being of students. Stephanie P. Jones (Spring 2020) in the article for *Teaching Tolerance* notes that the word "violence" is important and intentional:

> when we reserve the word violent as a descriptor for physical violence only, we fail to recognize the many ways in which non-physical injury happens, is normalized, and in the case of destructive pedagogy, harms students' learning and how they see themselves in it.
>
> (p. 47)

Jones created the database *Mapping Racial Trauma in Schools* to capture and closely examine how harm happens in schools and through curriculum. While Jones notes that there are other ways in which Black and Brown children experience racial trauma in schools (e.g., physical harm, online or cyberbullying, intimidation), curriculum trauma is almost never formally reported. Oftentimes, we are made aware of moments that involve curriculum trauma if a student or family posts about it on social media or draws attention to an incident.

In conversation with some college students who were reflecting on their K-12 experiences, many reflected on simulations and experiential learning that brought on racial trauma as a result of class activities. For example, even in 2026, there are reports of students having to reenact a slave auction. The students shared that, while maybe well-intended, the simulations caused a great deal of anxiety. Multiple students shared they were asked to participate in a South African apartheid simulation and Ellis Island immigration processes. These simulations often occur without deeper historical contexts, criticality, nor examples of resistance.

One way that teachers can mitigate curricular violence is to develop consistent habits of interrogating their practice. When examining their lessons and overall curricular units, teachers can ask, "Does this material present a single version of the story? Are examples of Black and Brown (or other minoritized identities) only told from the perspective of trauma? What examples and opportunities for criticality can I include that allow students to examine a particular experience?" Rather than simply accept what is given to us in standardized curriculum, we must continue to be critical of the ways in which curricular violence impacts student learning and the opportunities we have to provide a more robust understanding of the world.

Curricular Joy

When I first heard the term "curricular joy," I was not entirely sure what this meant. Did it mean I could only teach good news? Did it mean I had to avoid hard histories and experiences? Over the course of my own learning, I grew to understand the true "joyousness" that can come from a curriculum that brings in multiple opportunities for learning. One of the most influential texts addressing the importance of joy in curriculum is *Unearthing Joy* by Gholdy Muhammad. It is one of my favorite books to teach in class and continues to be one that the students identify as positively disrupting the field of education. Muhammad moves us from thinking only about skills as the primary input of curriculum development and pushes us to include aspects of identity, criticality, joy, and intellect. I ask my students to take existing standards, identify the skills that tend to be the outcomes of those standards, and then push them to create opportunities for identity, criticality, joy, and intellect. I have appreciated what Muhammad has done – giving students their own critical frameworks for disrupting positivist outcomes and being much more comprehensive about curriculum development.

Because the courses I teach are always focused on teacher-leader identity, we spend a considerable amount of time exploring how our own identities inform and impact how we approach the work of skills, identity, criticality, and joy. Students share how their past socialization in education shapes the kinds of change they want to see and make in education. By implementing an identity-conscious lens in this work, the students themselves bring their whole identities and experiences into the classroom discussion. And they, too, engage with criticality about what they have learned, seen, and experienced.

During critical check-ins, I ask the students, "On a scale of 1 [not very] to 10 [very], how often did you experience joy in your K-12 education and schooling?" The answers are mixed and range from 1 to somewhere around 8 or 9. The discussions that critical check-ins prompt are very telling. One student, Laney, a Black woman, stated that she grew up in a predominantly Black school environment that included Black teachers and leaders. Laney felt very affirmed, and many of the lessons were taught from a Black-centric and pro-Black perspective. When Laney went to a predominantly White college after K-12, she experienced culture shock when she realized that not everyone experienced school the same way. Undergraduate schooling was the first time she realized that others learned a very different curriculum – one in which whiteness was considered most powerful. "How would you describe your joy during this time?" I asked Laney. "Yeah, not joyful. College was when I realized that other people did not learn the same things that I learned, and they certainly were not learning those things in college either. It made me grateful for the community that surrounded me and chose, intentionally, what I should learn as a young Black student."

For many students, especially those who can attend college, higher education can be a time when they are exposed to new topics, curriculum, and instructors who focus on very specific areas of study as opposed to generalists. When asked, "Why do you love college so much?" Jay, a sophomore, answered, "College has been an opportunity for me to learn from a curriculum that is not centered on test taking and state standards. Because of this, my professors do not rush our learning nor the processes to get there. Different from high school, when I was curious about something slightly off topic or if the subject in class was making me think of a different connection, the teacher would always reply, 'I wish we could cover that, Jay, but we just don't have time.' Nearly every time I have asked a curious question in college, the professor has always responded with 'Interesting question! Let's stay here for a few minutes and hear what others think about that question.'" Jay was quick to reply that the institutions of schooling and the pressures to adhere to test standards were often the barriers to teachers following the lead of students. "Many times," Jay continued, "it really did seem like my high school teachers wanted to cover different material or provide more context for a situation, but they just didn't have the support to do so."

So how do we bring in curricular joy to our work? I return to teacher identity. It is true, as Jay mentioned earlier, that there are external and institutional pressures that can create barriers to doing what Muhammad suggests – providing opportunities for criticality, identity, intellect, joy, and skills. Teachers, those who are responsible for presenting and engaging with the curriculum, have opportunities to bring their own personal lens into the work and recognize their own areas of deficit. We can continue to push for more inclusive policies related to curriculum, be a part of the decision making process or at least voice our opinions about the curriculum, and push for more inclusive standards when selecting curriculum.

Power and Curriculum

While individual and institutional advocacy are important, I would be remiss if I did not address the policy, politics, and power behind curriculum and curricular choices. If we know that providing these opportunities creates better conditions for learning, then why are our current policies not aligning with these practices? As many educational scholars have noted, standards are often connected to capitalism. Districts and states (and organizations like the College Board) determine what the standards are for a content area subject, tests are created to measure competence in those subjects' areas, curriculum is designed to cover material on the tests, and the amount that teachers cover helps students prepare for the tests. Until we find ways to detangle learning from states that profit from standardized testing, we will continue to struggle with creating curriculum that addresses criticality, identity, intellect, joy, and skills and simply focus on the overly emphasized and limited skills measurement.

Activist-educator Tricia Ebarvia encourages teachers to consistently audit their curriculum and ask key questions: 1) In what ways is your curriculum shaped by your own educational experiences? 2) Whose voices are centered in the texts you teach? 3) Whose voices are marginalized or missing? 4) How do you recognize and celebrate the backgrounds of diverse authors already included in your curriculum? And 5) in what ways do you integrate cultural and racial literacy in your instruction? (Ebarvia, n.d.). By including Ebarvia's questions in our work towards curricular joy, we embrace that the curriculum must represent a range of identities, perspectives, and interactions beyond a Eurocentric or single-story approach. Doing so aligns our work with criticality, a reduction of harm, and an environment that welcomes joy.

Activities for Identity-Conscious Curriculum

Activity 1: 5-Minute Writing Prompts

To build community in a peer learning group, these 5-minute writing prompts are helpful ways to engage in reflection about curriculum. These prompts can be used 1) solely as a reflective exercise in a journal, 2) a think-write-pair-share, and/or 3) a large group share-out.

Prompt #1: As you think back to your education and schooling, what was a topic, subject, or lesson that you felt very engaged in? Why do you remember this? Be as descriptive as possible. How does identity inform and impact this engagement?

Prompt #2: If you were to design a curriculum based on your own passions and interests, what would you create? Why did you choose this? What do you hope your students would learn, experience, or feel because of this curriculum you created?

Prompt #3: Think about either your favorite or least favorite subject/area of study in school. Write a five-line poem based on how you felt about this subject area.

Prompt #4: What is something you wish you had more opportunities to learn about in your schooling? Why do you think that was not taught or not taught enough? What would have been different if you had the opportunity to learn more about this experience in your curriculum?

Activity 2: Getting Ready for Curriculum Work

While there are many frameworks for putting together lessons, units, and curriculum, one missing step is the opportunity to reflect on your own thoughts, attitudes, and feelings about identity-conscious curriculum. Use this activity as an important first step in examining some of your earliest messages about curriculum.

1. Reflecting on when you were the age range of your students (e.g., elementary school, middle, junior high, high school, college), what do you recall about how identity was addressed in your school curriculum?
2. When you think about the age range of your students, which of the identity categories (see list on pages 36–37) do you believe they are "too young" to talk about? Why do you believe that? What messages were you given about those topics and age appropriateness?
3. What identity topics are you most comfortable talking about with others? Why?
4. What identity topics do you want to talk more about with your students but may need some help or support in doing so?
5. As you build your awareness of experiences and ideas from different identity groups, please use this space to list a few of the identity categories and one or two books, resources, or texts you might access to inform your knowledge.

Activity 3: The Immersive Art Exhibit

Imagine your curriculum as an immersive art exhibit. Imagine your curriculum to be filled with visual images, sounds, textures, smells, and even feelings. Taking small chunks of your curriculum material (i.e., don't do this all during one sitting!), begin to write down where and how identity shows up in your curriculum.

- **What do your students see related to identity?** *In this section on famous writers, I have visual images of the different authors we are covering. Because I am interested in focusing on race and gender in this section, the images include many different people of color as well as women.*
- **What do your students hear related to identity?** *With the books we are covering, I have key moments of "read-aloud" for students to hear the cadence of different types of writing and even some of the words that are not translated in English. I validate that all languages are meaningful and valid.*

- **What can your students physically connect to in your curriculum related to identity?** *At the end of the unit, I ask the students to select five to eight of their most memorable lines or words from the books we read. Then they create their own scrapbook along with why those phrases or words meant something to them and how those words connected to their own lives.*
- **What areas come to life in your curriculum related to identity?** *After each book, the students write a reflection about which characters or storyline was a mirror to their experiences – something that felt familiar. They are then asked to write a reflection about which characters or storyline served as a window to a new experience – something that they learned or understand better now that they have read the text.*
- **What feelings does this lesson or section evoke for your students?** *My goal is for the students to experience a range of feelings. I want some of these stories to feel familiar to them, and I also want some of these stories to feel very unfamiliar to them. This helps them to see that the world both includes them and is also much bigger than them.*

Activity 4: Building an Identity-Conscious Lesson

If you are in the process of enhancing or integrating aspects of identity into your lesson plans, use this five-step model for identifying and developing critical questions for students.

Step 1: Complete your proximity map from Section 1. This gives you an idea of what identities and experiences you might be paying close attention to and what identities and experiences you might leave out simply because you are not proximate to them.

Step 2: If you are working with an existing curriculum or lesson plan, highlight existing areas that are related to identity.

Step 3: Next, mark areas where lessons or examples related to identity can be integrated. If there are no such areas, identify one or two ways you might integrate identity into the existing lesson.

Step 4: Using your proximity map, select identities you may want to integrate into those areas. Be mindful that you have identities and experiences that you are close to, that are important but sometimes get lost in your focus, and ones that you almost never think of or consider.

Step 5: Using a critical media lens (i.e., being mindful of your sources), look up resources, have conversations, and view videos that are related to this topic. Center age appropriateness. Develop an activity, discussion question, or query that students can use to develop critical thinking skills related to your lesson with an identity-conscious lens.

Activity 5: Rubric for Identity-Conscious Curriculum

In addition to content and subject specific rubrics you might use to select, enhance, or change your curriculum, this identity-conscious rubric provides helpful reflection questions about our own behaviors and approaches related to teaching, learning, and curricular choices.

Identity-Conscious Curriculum **Students are presented with a sequence of planned experiences and content that are aligned with standards.**	**Building Knowledge (I need to gather information about these areas.)** 1 | 2 | 3	**Engaging in Reflection (I am actively connecting how these areas are informed and impacted by my own identities.)** 4 | 5 | 6	**Implementing Action (I am using the knowledge and reflection to create actionable steps towards identity consciousness.)** 7 | 8 | 9
Theoretical Frameworks: I use theories to inform how I build or use curriculum.			
Identity-Conscious Curriculum: the content and planned activities share different perspectives, identities, and experiences.			
Culturally Relevant Curriculum: the content and sequence include different perspectives and disrupt a single-story approach to learning.			
Curricular Joy: the content and sequence of experiences provide students the opportunity to be critical about the content and their lived experiences			
Advocacy: I regularly assess the curriculum for ways in which identity is missing, and I advocate at the departmental, school, and district level for greater inclusion.			

Part IV Discussion Questions

With a peer learning group, discuss the following questions:

1. What aspects of this section validated your current experiences related to curriculum? Which aspects pushed or challenged your own thinking and doing related to curriculum?
2. What aspects of this section felt possible to do with your own curriculum? What aspects of this section felt difficult/challenging to do with your own curriculum?
3. From your experience, what have been the challenges or obstacles you have faced individually to developing a more identity-conscious curriculum?
4. From your experience, what challenges or obstacles have you faced institutionally to developing a more identity-conscious curriculum?
5. What collaborations exist (or need to be created) to support a more identity-conscious curriculum?

Part V

Bringing It All Together

Key elements

- What are some of the challenges for bringing together teaching, learning, and curriculum from an identity-conscious lens?
- What are some frequently asked questions and responses that might be helpful in guiding this journey?
- What can I do to continue to build habits and skills for engaging in teaching, learning, and curriculum from an identity-conscious lens?

Having taken a journey through this book by building knowledge, engaging in reflection, and moving to action, I hope you have had the chance to examine the conditions through which you developed thoughts, attitudes, behaviors, and beliefs about teaching, learning, and curriculum. Because identity informs and impacts everything we do, I imagine you also thought about how your identity (and the identities of others) shaped your educational journey too. Writing this book during a political climate that is openly hostile to identity work, I appreciate the challenges that have come with integrating conversations, lessons, and experiences related to identity. At its core, identity work is belonging work. And when we feel safe in a space where we belong, we can learn more effectively. Learning effectively, particularly when we take an identity-conscious approach, helps us

DOI: 10.4324/9781003784739-6

to build curiosity, collaboration, critical thinking skills, compassion, and stronger communities. It is not an easy task, but identity-conscious practices allow us to embrace the complexities of teaching, learning, and curriculum in ways that honor the diverse identities and experiences we all bring to our work.

Challenges in Bringing It All Together

Knowing that the current political and social climate can be hostile to identity work, I have compiled some of the most frequently asked questions that I get when teachers and school leaders want to lean into this work but worry about the pushback. It is important to remember that leadership matters here. Leadership can be a school committee, Board of Trustees, administrative team, parent councils, and policymakers. But courageous leadership, one that knows how to manage conflict effectively, is what can make the difference here. Challenges are an opportunity for growth. Leaders who approach these challenges with creativity, honesty, transparency, and courage can effectively shape communities of belonging. However, leaders who are risk-averse, who do not know how to manage conflict effectively, and who tend to take an all-or-nothing approach to the work find themselves moving away from identity-conscious teaching, learning, and curriculum. And when they move away from that, they move away from communities of belonging.

Too many decades of research have demonstrated that schools and classrooms are a place where discourse should occur. Discourse allows us the opportunity for critical thinking, for developing our opinions, and for rooting them in historical and social contexts. Though some critics of identity-conscious learning have misinterpreted this work to be "indoctrination," it is important to remember that exposure to different views, opinions, and stories allow learners to discern critical ideas. Exposure to the truth of our history, society, and challenges provides learners with the opportunities to grow and develop in a more holistic manner.

As you view some of these frequently asked questions, you will note a similar theme: leadership matters and differences matter. Schools and systems need to be clear about their mission, vision, and values to guide the work of identity-conscious teaching, learning, and curriculum.

Frequently Asked Question	What's Behind the Question	My Typical Response
Will I get in trouble for talking about identity in the classroom?	Many teachers worry about their employment security and the kinds of risks they are willing to take in the classroom. Some fear being targeted by parents, councils, or local advocacy groups interested in stopping this work.	"Particularly during these times, the worry and fear can be very real. You'll want to have an explicit conversation with your team leader (e.g., department chair, grade level leader, principal, head of school) to get a sense of what they believe is allowed given the school's climate. Work together to demonstrate that you know what is age appropriate and what works best for your students and classroom."
Doesn't talking about identity just highlight our differences when we should be focusing on our similarities?	There is an assumption here that "different" equals "bad." When we approach "different" as an opportunity to learn, we build strong global skills for curiosity, critical thinking, collaboration, and compassion.	"Many of us have learned that different = bad. But what if we approached these lessons from the mindset that difference allows us to have more interesting conversations together? We get to ask 'why' questions and see connections in our own lives."
I teach math. Conversations about identity do not naturally fit into my content. Do I really need to force it?	Many of us were socialized to believe that identity and humanity are only talked about in the social sciences. It is a learning curve to see how identity shows up in everything that we do, learn, and teach. The reality is that every subject, field, and discipline has had contributions by people of different identities. We should be including those different perspectives rather than just one way of knowing.	"I don't want you to force conversations about identity. But I think it's responsible to give our students a more full picture of content like math. For example, math's early history was rooted in what we call the Middle East. There are mathematicians to highlight who are women, people of color, people with disabilities, etc. Giving information about diverse types of mathematicians is one way to make your curriculum more identity-conscious. In addition, changing up the context of your problem sets – for example, in another part of the world where students must research the local area and the context through which they understand mathematics – is a great way to stimulate critical thinking."
I already must cover so much content. To add new lessons on identity would distract us from what I need to cover for the students to pass the test.	There is an overwhelming feeling that comes with adding identity-talk into the curriculum because people treat it like an add-on. Rather, teach the content through the lens of a different perspective.	"Learning the information from different perspectives can help strengthen the learning process for our students. Therefore, I plan on adding an accessible resource or perspective to engage critical thinking skills for my students in an area we are currently covering."

Frequently Asked Question	What's Behind the Question	My Typical Response
My students are so tired of talking about diversity. They say that we as a school are overdoing it, and they are experiencing diversity fatigue.	It is true that today's students have had significantly more exposure to diverse viewpoints, cultures, and experiences. And it is true that some schools do not have an effective scope and sequence for this. However, that doesn't mean we stop altogether. Identity and experiences should be woven into the existing lessons rather than simply be treated as a "special day or event."	"I agree that you all have been engaging with diversity throughout your school experience. Knowing that it's important to talk about differences and cultures and experiences, what recommendations would you make to improve HOW we do this work together?"
Our school is already doing identity work in the advisory curriculum. That means I don't have to add it to mine, right?	Many schools do utilize advisory time to engage in social and emotional learning opportunities. Yet we know that effective learning occurs across disciplines.	"Identity work that is siloed into one area is less effective than across the curriculum. It's great that they are having conversations about identity in advisory but that's just one area of the student's day. If we integrate identity-informed lessons throughout the curriculum, students can engage in more robust critical thinking about the impact of identity more broadly in their lives."
I'm worried about teaching about other types of identities when I don't share those experiences. Is it appropriate for me to do that?	Many teachers believe that we only can "teach what we know." Yet teaching is also about curiosity and collaboration. Approaching these types of opportunities with humility and curiosity is one helpful way to engage in identity work.	"I want to address the obvious: we are here in a class where we will read young adult Black authors, and I, as your teacher, am not Black. However, I trust that together, we can model curiosity and collaboration together as we explore impactful literature and contributions by Black authors in this class."
I have a very homogenous classroom with no diversity. Why would I bring up other identities if no one in my class can relate?	This statement comes from an assumption that only minoritized people benefit from diversity lessons. In fact, when classrooms are homogenous, there is less opportunity to engage with diverse perspectives, and therefore, it becomes even more important to introduce different perspectives and ideas into the classroom discussion.	"Our current classroom, school, and town are not as (racially) diverse as the rest of the country or world. Therefore, for us to understand how life is experienced outside of our bubble, we need opportunities to learn about different perspectives, views, and lives so that we have a more inclusive approach to the world."

Frequently Asked Question	What's Behind the Question	My Typical Response
The existing curriculum that we use does not have identity-based lessons. Does that mean I have to do my own research and add them in?	For consistency, many school districts purchase ready-made curriculum. While this can help with planning and preparation, these one-size-fits-all lessons do not always reflect the different identities in our classrooms or schools. Yes, it may mean that a teacher or instructional coach might have to find additional resources. It is important to remember, however, that we are not focused on "identity-based lessons" but that our lessons are identity-conscious and include a wide range of identities and experiences.	"I'm looking for some support and assistance with how to take my current lesson plan and make sure there is representation from diverse perspectives. I'd like to keep the same structure that was offered in the curriculum guide but include stories of women, people living with disabilities, single-parent families, and people of color. Are there some simple things I can do to provide some more windows and mirrors for my students in this lesson?"
In my class, students group themselves by different identities – for example, the girls sit together, the Black students sit together, and the international students from China sit together. Is this bad?	It is important to understand that this is not always a negative outcome. Sometimes students seek opportunities to be near those who help them feel comfortable. If this is happening in class, it could benefit learning if students are more comfortable in those groups, able to communicate more easily with each other, and engage in the lessons. However, it is also important to give students opportunities to learn in different groups and from each other. Make sure to scaffold that experience by providing directions and questions in advance and offering that you will be present to offer support during the activity. This may help to decrease some anxiety about the activity that day.	"I wanted to let you know ahead of time that on Wednesday, we will be mixing up the groups a bit for this one activity. I will make sure I have clear directions and instructions about what we are doing, will send them to you in advance, and give you time to prepare for your mixed-group work before it happens. I'll be in the room while you are all working together to answer questions, provide support, and even help you with some preparations in advance if you need it."

Frequently Asked Question	What's Behind the Question	My Typical Response
No one else on my teaching team wants to talk about identity, but I do. How do I do this without upsetting my colleagues?	First, you aren't alone. I have heard this from a few teachers who are very invested in shaping a community of belonging but who are working with others (or on teams) for whom this is not a priority. Bring up the topic of wanting to teach in a more identity-conscious way and see what reactions you get. Offer up an example of how you will do this (ideally not overhauling the curriculum) and help them see that it is doable. Invite colleagues to view your lesson in real time to demonstrate how it works. Sometimes people are hesitant because they are fearful of the unknown and how it will work out.	"When we do the read-aloud tomorrow, I've decided to read from two different books with similar topics. They are two books about how different families celebrate the winter holidays. One is a Christmas book and the other is a Hanukkah book. "I'm going to ask the students: 1) What did you notice about these two books? And 2) what is similar about these two families? And 3) what was different about these two families? "I want to show students that families celebrate in different ways but that there are similar themes in these stories. If your class would like to join, I'd be happy to make some room!"
Is it true that there have been teachers who have been fired for having a gay pride flag in their room or signs that say, "We all belong"?	In this current political climate, there has been external pressure to eliminate any conversations related to identity and belonging in schools. Yet, as educators, we know how important it is to create an environment where all students feel safe. Unfortunately, there have been districts that have approached this by disciplining or censuring teachers. So, yes, this has occurred. And districts and school leaders should clarify what they are willing to do to both support students and address the pressure.	"It would be helpful for us teachers to hear from the school leadership and district administration about what you currently will support or not support on behalf of teachers. This will allow us to have clear guidelines about what we can do in our classrooms, how we can impact belonging, and how we can keep ourselves safe."

Frequently Asked Question	What's Behind the Question	My Typical Response
A parent emailed me and asked me to send to them, in advance, any lessons that talk about identity before I teach them. Do I need to do this?	Parents and caregivers are often operating out of care and concern for their children. Sometimes, this can come across as micromanaging and getting too involved in the daily work of a teacher. And teachers do operate with a level of autonomy in most schools and have been trusted to teach age-appropriate lessons in their work. It is important to get clarity from your school leadership about what the expectation is here that both honors your autonomy and helps to engage the parents/caregivers.	"Dear xxxx, thank you for your note. I would like to learn more about what you may be looking for in these lessons. I am also checking in with Principal xxxx, who can advise me about what is expected in a strong home-and-school connection and how to best support this relationship."

Overall, it is important to remember that education is conflict work. As teachers and school leaders, we know that conflict can be an opportunity for growth. Without conflict or challenge, we stay the same. This pressure allows us to examine why we do what we do and refine it, if needed. Identity work is complicated and complex because identity work is *people work*. And *people* are complicated and complex. If you can embrace that this work is challenging and that challenge leads to change, then you are on the right path!

Intersections of Teaching, Learning, and Curriculum

Though this book has addressed teaching, learning, and curriculum as three separate parts, it is clear they are deeply connected. Additionally, because we are viewing these parts through an identity-conscious lens, we are honoring the complexity of the work.

I often hear that one of the challenges to making changes is *time. Liza, there is no time in the schedule. Liza, there is no time to do professional development. Liza, there is no time during faculty meetings to do this kind of work. Liza, I'm exhausted at the end of a very difficult teaching day, and there isn't time to do this work afterwards.*

All true.

I agree that if schools do not make the time – carve out realistic time for this work – it will not get done. One of my favorite quotes from Zaretta Hammond is "We cannot PD (professional development) our way out of this." We cannot simply rely on the good will of teachers nor whether they have enough energy at the end of a long day to do additional work to carry this forward. Schools need to make institutional commitments by creating realistic time and space for this work. This can be time set aside during faculty meetings, time during quarterly professional development days, or providing grade-level or departmental teams time during the school day to work collaboratively (and not during a designated prep period). This could look, for example, like the 3rd-grade team using a "retreat" day while their students are working on a special program day.

It is also important to remember that identity-conscious practices are not about completely throwing away your existing teaching, learning, and curriculum models. The work is about integrating identity and making space for it. When we ask ourselves, "How, if at all, does identity show up in this section?" then we can begin to address an identity-conscious practice. What are small changes you can make in your reading list? Your problem set? The examples that you give when highlighting researchers or scientists? If you are teaching a lesson on comparing historical documents, are you only including White authors or are you bringing in other voices to diversify perspectives in the curriculum? Do you have opportunities to also talk about decolonizing practices or how power dictates whose story is told?

Identity-conscious practices are not an add-on. They are an integrated part of *how* we teach, not just *what* we teach. Identity-conscious practices begin as skills and, with consistency, develop into habits. Soon, you realize you are no longer "adding on" identity-consciousness but are beginning with it. You start to create lesson plans with identity in mind. You begin framing assessments that are rooted in culturally responsive learning styles. You facilitate classroom discussions by leading with trauma-informed practices. If you continue to build these habits and skills of an identity-conscious teaching, learning, and curricular practices, it just becomes the way you do things.

Activities For Bringing It All Together

Activity 1: Templates and Action Plans

Now that you have gone through the experience of examining an identity-conscious teaching, learning, and curriculum (ICTLC) approach, use this template to develop an action plan for how you will move forward. Recognize areas of strength and opportunities, and identify what supports you will need moving forward.

	Something I understand very well about this practice	Something I need to learn more about to engage further	One action I can take to move my actions forward	One person, resource, or guide that can support my next steps
Identity-Consciousness				
Teaching				
Learning				
Curriculum				

Activity 2: Moving from Skills to Habits

In this work, you have learned that we build skills that turn into habits. Using the following grid, begin to outline how the skills you learn related to identity-conscious teaching, learning, and curriculum can slowly become habits in your practice.

Skill I want to work on	A daily action I can do to support this skill	A weekly action I can do to support this skill	A monthly action I can do to support this skill
Reflective practice for myself related to my teaching	*At the end of each day, I can write down what I believe went well in my teaching and where I felt challenged.*	*At the end of the five days (M–F) of reflection, I can select one challenge that I'd like to focus on for improvement in the following week.*	*I can use the rubrics in the book (teaching, learning, and curriculum) and identify where I might be after a month of both reflective practice and identifying areas of challenge.*

Activity 3: Theory-Informed Practice

Throughout this book, you have had the opportunity to learn about different theories related to identity-conscious practice, teaching, learning, and curriculum. As educators, we are often seeking connections between theory and practice. Using the following prompts, identify how you will operationalize the different theories provided in this book as you build the habits and skills of identity-conscious practices.

1. First, select one of the areas you would like to focus on as we move from theory to practice: identity, teaching, learning, and curriculum.
2. Next, identify one of the theories discussed in this book or one that you want to bring into the exercise.
3. Then chunk the theory into smaller pieces so that you can begin aligning action steps. Which part of the theory or theoretical framework would you like to pay attention to?
4. Finally, what actions correspond to that part of the theory? What does that part of the theory look like in practice?

Example:

1. *I want to focus on theories related to my teaching practice.*
2. *I want to better understand critical race theory and its application to my teaching.*
3. *I am interested in this interpretation of "interest convergence" – that people tend to do things that they also benefit from. That rarely do people just do things "because it's the right thing to do," but rather, there is this theory that there must be something "in it for them."*
4. *I realize that my students at this age group are still quite egocentric and connect to things that have to do with them. Despite wanting them to "do the right thing" on its own, I realize that interest convergence provides a lens to understand that, related to race, people will do things if they find there is a benefit to them too.*
5. *I want to start integrating books that have complicated situations. I want students to not only think about what they would do in these scenarios but also what benefit looks like. I want to unmask both how interest convergence explains some of the hesitation that White people face when engaging in race and identity work and provide opportunities for the students to think critically about what they would do in situations.*

Part V Discussion Questions

With a peer learning group, discuss the following questions:

1. What aspects of this book affirmed what you already knew about identity-conscious teaching, learning, and curriculum (ICTLC)?
2. What aspects of this book challenged your thinking about identity-conscious teaching, learning, and curriculum (ICTLC)?
3. How might a peer learning community support you in being accountable to your action steps?
4. What action steps have you identified to bring together teaching, learning, curriculum, and identity?
5. What institutional barriers do you face in engaging with an identity-conscious teaching, learning, and curriculum practice (ICTLC)?
6. What is one thing you are curious or wondering about as you begin your identity-conscious journey?

Conclusion

We know that identity informs and impacts how we act, interact, and see the world around us. We also know that teaching, learning, and curriculum are key parts of the educational landscape. Yet we have not always approached teaching, learning, and curriculum from an identity-conscious lens. Doing so allows us to fully lean into our own humanity as teachers, into the lives of our students as learners, and to partner more closely with our schools through curriculum.

During the writing of this book, we have witnessed major changes in education in the United States due to executive orders, policies, and government reductions in departments such as the Department of Education, including services for students with disabilities. During the writing of this book, there were nationwide protests pushing back against bans on educational research, science funding, and international grants. Professors lost research funds, labs closed, and scholars were impacted by fears of visas not being approved. Quickly, other countries recognized the barriers that the United States was putting up related to the advancement of scholarship and research and began offering admission to their universities to scholars who were not coming back to the United States from abroad. These decisions were informed and impacted by identity – by race, country of origin, political identities and ideologies, and even research interests.

To look at the educational landscape and not see how identity is impacted is shortsighted. As educators, we must collectively lean into our work in teaching, learning, and curriculum in addition to leadership, decision making, and

DOI: 10.4324/9781003784739-7

policy for education to continue to be a place of discourse and discovery. While the research, activities, discussion questions, and rubrics help us build healthy habits and skills for important dialogue about our field and our work, we cannot give up. We must continue to commit to doing what we do and know best – that schools are a place of learning new ideas, of being presented with opportunities to think critically, and of building communities of thinkers and doers who will make decisions with all the information possible.

As educators, we are facing challenging times. But our profession has not only been at the center of change; we have a responsibility to teach through the changing landscape and provide our students, families, and ourselves the best pathways for critical thinking. As of the final draft of this book in early February 2026, the Department of Education dropped its appeal to a federal ruling that had blocked its efforts to restrict diversity, equity, and inclusion in schools, colleges, and universities. In essence, that meant the past year of restrictions against diversity, equity, and inclusion initiatives were unenforceable. The administration had threatened to revoke federal funding for any schools that were engaging in DEI work, and this was no longer the standard. While this is a major victory towards returning to an identity-conscious practice in terms of legality, there is still public opinion against DEI work. Largely, I believe this public opinion was intentionally misinformed and misled. The rhetoric around identity and DEI work was used to stoke fear, anxiety, and lean into some of the most painful moments of our history.

People often ask me, "Liza, how can you continue to do this identity work given all the pressures, pushback, and anger related to the work?" My answer has remained consistent in its simplicity: "I know what happens when we don't continue." I am a product of an educational system that did not value my identity as a person of color, child of immigrants, and an Asian American. I am the product of an educational system that taught me of White superiority while simultaneously only exposing me to a curriculum that were limited to narratives of Black inferiority. I was taught that colonizing land, countries, and people were the destinies of White explorers all while erasing the stories, histories, and culture of people who were original to the land.

Intervention, for me, did not happen until college. I was 19 years old as a college undergraduate when I was first exposed to a more critically situated narrative of people, history, and culture. And I was 42 years old and in my doctoral program when I first learned about the atrocities and violence perpetuated against Native and Indigenous children of this land. My values related to transparency, truth, and amplification of these voices drives why I teach, learn, and build curriculum rooted in identity-conscious practices. I show up this way because I was the product of an identity-absent teaching, learning, and curricular environment. I grew up not knowing the truth. I grew up not having the opportunities to engage with discourse, to think critically, and to question what I was learning.

I often end my workshops with "Be the person your younger self needed." My younger self needed someone who saw me. My younger self needed someone who believed there was more than just one story out there. My younger self needed someone who understood how teaching, learning, and curriculum shape not only the skills we learn today but also the habits we build in the future.

I am grateful you chose this book and this journey to critically examine our own teaching, learning, and curricular practices particularly in today's educational landscape. When you are feeling discouraged or are not sure where this is all going, I encourage you to remember the point of an identity-conscious practice. The purpose of an identity-conscious practice is to engage with curiosity, collaboration, critical thinking, compassion, and community. All these components – these values – contribute to a healthier and more vibrant teaching, learning, and curricular experience. But you do not have to do this alone. You are among a community of teachers, learners, and leaders who know that identity matters and that by building habits and skills for an identity-conscious practice, we demonstrate a commitment to not only education but also to each other.

References

Allen, K.-A., Slaten, C. D., Arslan, G., Roffey, S., Craig, H., & Vella-Brodrick, D. A. (2022). School belonging: The importance of student and teacher relationships. In M. L. Kern & M. L. Wehmeyer (Eds.), *The Palgrave handbook of positive education* (pp. 525–550). Palgrave Macmillan/Springer Nature. https://doi.org/10.1007/978-3-030-64537-3_21

Annamma, S., Connor, D., & Ferri, B. (2013). Dis/ability critical race studies (DisCrit): Theorizing at the intersections of race and dis/ability. *Race Ethnicity and Education*, *16*(1), 1–31. https://doi.org/10.1080/13613324.2012.730511

Armstrong-Carter, E. (2023). Why the U.S. must recognize and support caregiving students in middle and high schools. *The Hechinger Report*. https://hechingerreport.org/opinion-why-the-u-s-must-recognize-and-support-caregiving-students-in-middle-and-high-schools/

Armstrong-Carter, E., Siskowski, C., Belkowitz, J., Johnson, C., & Olson, E. (2022). Child and adolescent caregiving for family: Emotional, social, physical, and academic risk and individual differences. *Journal of Family Psychology*, *36*(8), 1407–1417. https://doi.org/10.1037/fam0000969

Atkinson, D. R., Morten, G., & Sue, D. W. (1993). *Counseling American minorities: A cross cultural perspective* (4th ed.). Brown and Benchmark.

Baptiste, S. A. (2010). *Moving beyond Black history month: How three teachers interpreted and implemented the New Jersey Amistad legislation*. Rutgers, the State University of New Jersey, School of Graduate Studies.

Barnum, M. (2017). New research may build discrimination case for widely used principals exam. *Medium*. https://the74million.medium.com/new-research-may-build-discrimination-case-for-widely-used-principals-exam-e4a937ece152

Bertrand, S. K., & Porcher, K. (2020). Teacher educators as disruptors redesigning courses in teacher preparation programs to prepare white preservice teachers. *Journal of Culture and Values in Education*, *3*(1), 72–88.

Bishop, R. S. (1990, March). *Windows and mirrors: Children's books and parallel cultures* (pp. 3–12). California State University Reading Conference: 14th Annual Conference Proceedings.

Blazar, D. (2024). Why black teachers matter. *Educational Researcher (Online First), 53*.

Bobbitt, F. (1918). *The curriculum*. Houghton Mifflin. https://www.ebsco.com/research-starters/social-sciences-and-humanities/curriculum-theory

Bottiani, J. H., Bradshaw, C. P., & Mendelson, T. (2017). A multilevel examination of racial disparities in high school discipline: Black and white adolescents' perceived equity, school belonging, and adjustment problems. *Journal of Educational Psychology, 109*(4), 532.

Brown, B. A., Boda, P., Lemmi, C., & Monroe, X. (2019). Moving culturally relevant pedagogy from theory to practice: Exploring teachers' application of culturally relevant education in science and mathematics. *Urban Education, 54*(6), 775–803.

Carter, P. L., Skiba, R., Arredondo, M. I., & Pollock, M. (2017). You can't fix what you don't look at: Acknowledging race in addressing racial discipline disparities. *Urban Education, 52*(2), 207–235.

Chandler-Ward, J., & Denevi, E. (2023). *Learning and teaching while White: Antiracist strategies for school communities*. Routledge.

Chang, M., & Kiang, P. (2002). *New challenges of representing Asian American students in higher education*. In W. Smith, P. Altbach, & K. Lomotey (Eds.), *Racial crisis in American higher education: Continuing challenges for the twenty-first century* (pp. 137–158). SUNY Press.

The Children's Bureau. (2023). *Child maltreatment 2023*. https://acf.gov/cb/report/child-maltreatment-2023

Crenshaw, K. W. (1988). Toward a race-conscious pedagogy in legal education. *National Black Law Journal, 11*, 1.

Crenshaw, K. W., Gotanda, N., Peller, G., & Thomas, K. (Eds.). (1995). *Critical race theory: The key writings that formed the movement*. The New Press.

Cross, W. E., Jr. (1971). The Negro-to-Black conversion experience. *Black World, 20*(9), 13–27.

Daus-Magbual, R. R. (2010). *Political, emotional, powerful: The transformative influence of the pin [at] y educational partnerships (PEP)*. University of San Francisco.

Directors of Health Promotion and Education (DHPE). (2005). *School employee wellness: A guide for protecting the assets of our nation's schools*. Washington, DC: Centers for Disease Control http://c.ymcdn.com/sites/www.dhpe.org/resource/group/75a95e00-448d-41c5-8226-0d20f29787de/Downloadable_Materials/EntireGuide.pdf.

Ebarvia, T. (n.d.). How inclusive is your literacy classroom really? *Heinemann Blog*.

Ferdman, B. M., & Gallegos, P. I. (2001). Racial identity development and Latinos in the United States. In C. L. Wijeyesinghe, & B. W. Jackson III (Eds.), *New perspectives on racial identity development: A theoretical and practical anthology* (pp. 32–66). New York University Press.

Fong, J. (2014). When this teacher's ethnic studies classes were banned, his students took the district to court – and won. *YES Magazine*.

Freire, P. (2000). *Pedagogy of the oppressed.* Continuum.

Garcia, S. B., & Guerra, P. L. (2004). Deconstructing deficit thinking: Working with educators to create more equitable learning environments. *Education and Urban Society, 36*(2), 150–168.

Gay, G. (2002). Preparing for culturally responsive teaching. *Journal of Teacher Education, 53*(2), 106–116.

Gay, G. (2010). *Culturally responsive teaching: Theory, research, and practice.* Teachers College Press.

Georgetown Psychology. (2025, December 22). Homework in elementary school: Does it really help students? *Georgetown Psychology.* https://georgetownpsychology.com/2025/12/studies-show-theres-minimal-academic-benefits-of-homework-in-elementary-school/

Glatthorn, A., Boschee, F., Whitehead, B. M., & Boschee, B. (2005). *Curriculum leadership: Development and implementation.* SAGE Publications.

González, N., Moll, L. C., Tenery, M. F., Rivera, A., Rendón, P., Gonzales, R., & Amanti, C. (2005). *Funds of knowledge: Theorizing practices in households, communities, and classrooms.* Mahwah, NJ: Lawrence Erlbaum Associates.

Gray, L., & Taie, S. (2015). *Public school teacher attrition and mobility in the first five years: Results from the first through fifth waves of the 2007–08 beginning teacher longitudinal study.* First Look. NCES 2015–337. National Center For Education Statistics.

Gregory, A., Skiba, R. J., & Noguera, P. A. (2010). The achievement gap and the discipline gap: Two sides of the same coin? *Educational Researcher, 39*(1), 59–68.

Hagerty, B. M., Williams, R. A., & Oe, H. (2002). Childhood antecedents of adult sense of belonging. *Journal of Clinical Psychology, 58*(7), 793–801.

Hammond, Z. (2014). *Culturally responsive teaching and the brain: Promoting authentic engagement and rigor among culturally and linguistically diverse students.* Corwin Press.

Hammond, Z. (2025). *Rebuilding students' learning power: Teaching for instructional equity and cognitive justice.* Corwin Press.

Helms, J. E. (1990). *Black and White racial identity: Theory, research, and practice.* Greenwood Press.

Helms, J. E., & Cook, D. A. (1999). *Using race and culture in counseling and psychotherapy: Theory and process.* Allyn & Bacon.

Horse, P. G. (2005). Native American identity. *New Directions for Student Services, 109.*

Howard-Hamilton, M. F. (2000). Creating a culturally responsive learning environment for African American students. *New Directions for Teaching and Learning, 2000*(82), 45–53.

Hu-DeHart, E. (1992, Spring–Summer). From yellow peril to model minority. *The New World, 1.*

Huenecke, D. (1982). What is curriculum theorizing? What are its implications for practice. *Educational Leadership, 39*(4), 290–294.

Ighodaro, E., & Wiggan, G. A. (2010). *Curriculum violence: America's new civil rights issue* (Vol. 27). Nova Science Publishers.

Iglesias, E. (1997). Forward: International law, human rights, and LatCrit theory. *University of Miami InterAmerican Law Review, 28*, 177–213.

Jones, S. P. (2020). Ending curriculum violence. *Teaching Tolerance, 64*(1), 47–50.

Kendi, I. X. (2023). *How to be an antiracist*. One World.

Kiang, P. N. (1999). *Long term effects of diversity in the curriculum: Analyzing the impact of Asian American studies in the lives of alumni from an urban commuter university* (Final Report). National Association of Student Personnel Administrators.

Kim, J. (1981). *Processes of Asian American identity development: A study of Japanese American women's perceptions of their struggle to achieve positive identities as Americans of Asian ancestry* (Doctoral Dissertation).

Knowles, M. S. (1968). Androgogy not pedagogy. *Adult Leadership, 16*(10), 350–352.

Kohn, A. (2012, October). *The case against homework*. Alfie Kohn. https://www.alfiekohn.org/article/case-against-homework/

Kokka, K. (2020). Social justice pedagogy for whom? Developing privileged students' critical mathematics consciousness. *The Urban Review, 52*(4), 778–803.

Kolluri, S., & Tichavakunda, A. A. (2023). The counter-deficit lens in educational research: Interrogating conceptions of structural oppression. *Review of Educational Research, 93*(5), 641–678.

Ladson-Billings, G. (1995). Toward a theory of culturally relevant pedagogy. *American Educational Research Journal, 32*(3), 465–491.

Ladson-Billings, G. (1998). Just what is critical race theory and what's it doing in a nice field like education? *International Journal of Qualitative Studies in Education, 11*(1), 7–24. https://doi.org/10.1080/095183998236863

Ladson-Billings, G. (2021). Three decades of culturally relevant, responsive, & sustaining pedagogy: What lies ahead? *The Educational Forum, 85*(4), 351–354. https://doi.org/10.1080/00131725.2021.1957632

Lever, N., Mathis, E., & Mayworm, A. (2017). School mental health is not just for students: Why teacher and school staff wellness matters. *Report on Emotional & Behavioral Disorders in Youth, 17*(1), 6.

Lin, M., Lake, V. E., & Rice, D. (2008). Teaching anti-bias curriculum in teacher education programs: What and how. *Teacher Education Quarterly, 35*(2), 187–200.

Losen, D. J., Hodson, C. L., Keith, M. A., II, Morrison, K., & Belway, S. (2015). *Are we closing the school discipline gap*? Teachers College Press.

Maryland State Education Association. (2017). *Trauma toolkit. Maryland State Education Association*. First Book.

Marzano, R. J. (2003). *What works in schools: Translating research into action.* ASCD.

Maslow, A. H. (1962). Some basic propositions of a growth and self-actualization psychology. *Perceiving, Behaving, Becoming: A New Focus for Education*, 34–49.

McLaughlin, C. (2016, April 20). *The homework gap: The "cruelest part of the digital divide"*. National Education Association. https://www.nea.org/nea-today/all-news-articles/homework-gap-cruelest-part-digital-divide

Michael, A., & Bartoli, E. (2014). What White children need to know about race. *Independent School, 73*(4), 56–62.

Muhammad, G. (2023). *Unearthing joy: A guide to culturally and historically responsive curriculum and instruction.* Scholastic Professional.

Murphy, M. C., & Zirkel, S. (2015). Race and belonging in school: How anticipated and experienced belonging affect choice, persistence, and performance. *Teachers College Record, 117*(12), 1–40.

Museus, S. D. (2008). The model minority and the inferior minority myths: Understanding stereotypes and their implications for student learning. *About Campus, 13*(3), 2–8.

Museus, S. D., & Iftikar, J. (2013). An Asian critical theory (AsianCrit) framework. *Asian American Students in Higher Education, 31*(10), 18–29.

Mutua, A. D. (2008). Introducing ClassCrits: From class blindness to a critical legal analysis of economic inequality. *Buffalo Law Review, 56*, 859.

National Center for Educational Statistics (NCES). (2016). https://nces.ed.gov/nhes/tables/homework_time.asp

National Center for Educational Statistics (NCES). (2021). https://nces.ed.gov/surveys/ntps/estable/table/ntps/ntps2021_sflt01_t1s

National Council on Teacher Quality. (2023). https://www.nctq.org/policy-area/teacher-diversity/

National Educators Association. (2019, November 10). *How much homework is too much*? National Education Association. https://www.nea.org/professional-excellence/student-engagement/tools-tips/how-much-homework-too-much

National Educators Association (NEA). (2026). Educator Pay Data for 2025. https://www.nea.org/resource-library/educator-pay-and-student-spending-how-does-your-state-rank

North Carolina State University. (1997). *Center for universal design.* College of Design. https://design.ncsu.edu/research/center-for-universal-design/

Oberle, E., & Schonert-Reichl, K. A. (2016). Stress contagion in the classroom? The link between classroom teacher burnout and morning cortisol in elementary school students. *Social Science & Medicine, 159*, 30–37. PubMed: 27156042.

Pew Research Center. (2024, April). *What's it like to be a teacher in America today?* https://www.pewresearch.org/social-trends/2024/04/04/teachers-job-satisfaction/

Phinney, J. S. (1990). Ethnic identity in adolescents and adults: Review of research. *Psychological Bulletin, 108*(3), 499–514. https://doi.org/10.1037/0033-2909.108.3.499

Poe, E. A. (1947). *The murders in the Rue Morgue.* Editorial Ink.

Pollard, D. S., & Ajirotutu, C. (2001). *Lessons from America: The African American immersion schools experiment.* In R. Majors (Ed.), *Educating our Black children: New directions and radical approaches* (pp. 79–89). New York: Routledge.

Porowski, A., O'Conner, R., & Passa, A. (2014). *Disproportionality in school discipline: An assessment of trends in Maryland, 2009–12* (REL 2014-017). Regional Educational Laboratory Mid-Atlantic.

Poston, W. S. C. (1990). The biracial identity development model: A needed addition. *Journal of Counseling and Development, 69,* 152–155.

Public Broadcasting System. (2001.) *Only a teacher.* https://www.pbs.org/onlyateacher/

Rosenberg, M., & McCullough, B. C. (1981). Mattering: Inferred significance and mental health among adolescents. *Research in Community & Mental Health,* 2, 163–182.

Rynders, D. (2019). Battling implicit bias in the IDEA to advocate for African American students with disabilities. *Touro Law Review, 35,* 461.

Sanders, F. C. (2009). *A curricular policy forty years in the making: The implementation of an African American history course in the Philadelphia school district* (Unpublished Doctoral Dissertation). The Pennsylvania State University.

Sandlin, J. A. (2005). Andragogy and its discontents: An analysis of andragogy from three critical perspectives. *PAACE Journal of Lifelong Learning, 14,* 25–42.

Schwab, J. J. (1973). The practical 3: Translation into curriculum. *The School Review, 81*(4), 501–522.

Sealey-Ruiz, Y. (2026). *Archaeology of self: The introspective educator's guide to racial literacy.* Taylor & Francis.

Skiba, R. J., Horner, R. H., Chung, C. G., Rausch, M. K., May, S. L., & Tobin, T. (2011). Race is not neutral: A national investigation of African American and Latino disproportionality in school discipline. *School Psychology Review, 40*(1), 85–107.

Sleeter, C. E. (2012). Confronting the marginalization of culturally responsive pedagogy. *Urban Education, 47*(3), 562–584.

Smith, E. J., & Harper, S. R. (2015). *Disproportionate impact of K-12 school suspension and expulsion on Black students in Southern states.* Philadelphia,

PA: Center for the Study of Race and Equity in Education, University of Pennsylvania Graduate School of Education.

Solórzano, D. G., & Yosso, T. J. (2002). Critical race methodology: Counter-storytelling as an analytical framework for education research. *Qualitative Inquiry*, *8*(1), 23–44.

Starck, J. G., Riddle, T., Sinclair, S., & Warikoo, N. (2020). Teachers are people too: Examining the racial bias of teachers compared to other American adults. *Educational Researcher*, *49*(4), 273–284.

Strayhorn, T. L. (2018). *College students' sense of belonging: A key to educational success for all students*. Routledge.

Talusan, L. A. (2016). *The formation of scholars: Critical narratives of Asian American and Pacific Islander doctoral students in higher education. University of Massachusetts*.

Talusan, L. A. (2022). *Identity-conscious educator: Building habits and skills for a more inclusive school*. Solution Tree Press.

Tatum, B. D. (2007). *Can we talk about race? And other conversations in an era of school resegregation*. Beacon Press.

Terlizzi, E., & Norris, T. (2021). *Mental health treatment among adults in 2020*. Department of Health and Human Services, Center for Disease Control.

Tillman, L. C. (2004). (Un) intended consequences? The impact of the Brown v. Board of Education decision on the employment status of Black educators. *Education and Urban Society*, *36*(3), 280–303.

Tintiangco-Cubales, A., Kiang, P. N. C., & Museus, S. (2010). Praxis and power in the intersections of education. *AAPI Nexus: Policy, Practice and Community*, *8*(1), v–xviii.

Tintiangco-Cubales, A., Kohli, R., Sacramento, J., Henning, N., Agarwal-Rangnath, R., & Sleeter, C. (2015). Toward an ethnic studies pedagogy: Implications for K-12 schools from the research. *The Urban Review*, *47*(1), 104–125.

The Trevor Project. (2024). https://www.thetrevorproject.org/survey-2024/

Tyler, R. (1949). *Basic principles of curriculum and instruction*. University of Chicago Press.

U.S. Bureau of Labor Statistics. (2024, August 19). *Employment population ratio 22.5 percent for high school students, 44.3 percent for college students*. Bureau of Labor Statistics. https://www.bls.gov/opub/ted/2024/employment-population-ratio-22-5-percent-for-high-school-students-44-3-percent-for-college-students.htm

Villegas, A. M., & Lucas, T. (2002). Preparing culturally responsive teachers: Rethinking the curriculum. *Journal of Teacher Education*, *53*(1), 20–32.

Vincent, C. G., Swain-Bradway, J., Tobin, T. J., & May, S. (2011). Disciplinary referrals for culturally and linguistically diverse students with and without disabilities: Patterns resulting from school-wide positive behavior support. *Exceptionality, 19*(3), 175–190.

Washington Post. (2020). Does homework work. *Washington Post.* https://www.washingtonpost.com/education/2020/09/01/does-homework-work-when-kids-are-learning-all-day-home/

Will, M. (2022, May 16). "Brown v. Board" decimated the Black educator pipeline: A scholar explains how. *Education Week.* https://www.edweek.org/teaching-learning/brown-v-board-decimated-the-black-educator-pipeline-a-scholar-explains-how/2022/05

Wood, J. T. (2008). Critical feminist theories. In L. A. Baxter, & D. O. Braithwaite (Eds.), *Engaging theories in interpersonal communication: Multiple perspectives* (pp. 323–334). Thousand Oaks, CA: SAGE Publications.

For Product Safety Concerns and Information please contact our EU representative GPSR@taylorandfrancis.com
Taylor & Francis Verlag GmbH, Kaufingerstraße 24, 80331 München, Germany

www.ingramcontent.com/pod-product-compliance
Lightning Source LLC
LaVergne TN
LVHW081937101026
849796LV00048B/434

9781041328292